Introduction

Diagraming is just one tool that can be used to facilita
the structure of language. For those students who learn best through physical manipulation, diagraming may well be the easiest way to understand syntax. Diagraming develops students' ability to see within sentences the structural relationships that they might otherwise miss.

Most importantly, diagraming is a process that forces students to think. Used as part of a thorough language-development program, sentence diagraming will add a component often missing: right brain directed activities. The greater the diversity in your language analysis presentation, the greater the chance of reaching the needs of all of your students.

Our goal is to make sure that students are never confronted with a sentence structure that is unfamiliar to them. *Diagraming*, Book 1 begins with simple (subject-verb) sentences and proceeds to subject-verb-complement sentences. *Diagraming*, Book 2 continues from that point and proceeds to more complex sentence structures.

How to Use

Most of the sentence diagraming in this workbook should be done on separate paper. Other directed activities may be done either in the book or on separate paper. The following directions apply to all exercises on the student worksheets.

Exercise 1

Have students follow the example models at the top of the page to diagram the given sentences. Make sure that they correctly identify the sentence parts before they diagram the sentences. If the students are wrongly identifying the parts, obviously the diagrams will be faulty.

Note: *The underlining of sentence parts will not be addressed in the Answer Key because of space limits. Refer to the diagrams for help in identifying the sentences parts.*

Exercise 2

The "Create a Sentence" exercise allows students to creatively address the specific diagraming structure they have just encountered. Students should be encouraged to have fun using their imaginations. These sentences could be shared with the class.

Exercise 3

The "Unscramble" exercise will frustrate some students and delight others. It forces students to try to visualize groups of words that might function as units, e.g., prepositional phrases. Suggest that students try their hand at scrambling some sentences of their own and then presenting them to the class.

Note: *The diagrams themselves will indicate the correct sentence structure.*

Exercise 4

This exercise provides the opportunity for students to recognize errors and to make corrections. Challenge the students to develop this type of exercise themselves. Students seem to delight in making "mistakes" on purpose.

Review Section

These exercises are to be used if the teacher feels extra practice is necessary. These exercises may also be used as a possible quiz or as a cooperative learning opportunity. For this reason, there is no answer key provided.

Note: Due to the topic's simplicity, the Simple Sentence (subject-verb) is not addressed in the Review Section.

Simple Sentences

Name________________________

Simple sentences (subject-verb) require a single horizontal line bisected by a vertical line which separates the subject from the verb. The articles *a, an,* and *the* are adjectives and are placed on a diagonal line beneath the noun(s) they modify.

Examples:

Trees sway.

Trees | sway

The birds can sing.

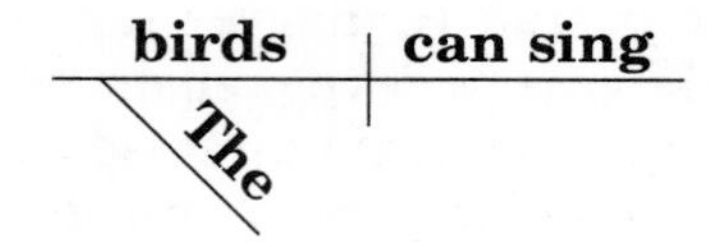

EXERCISE 1

In the following sentences, underline the subjects once and the verbs twice. Then diagram the sentences.

1. Dogs run.
2. Cats climb.
3. The fish swim.
4. Snakes slide.
5. A duck quacks.
6. The salamanders slither.
7. Dinosaurs rumble.
8. Badgers burrow.
9. The hyena yelps.
10. Giraffes can run.

EXERCISE 2

Create sentences to fit these diagrams. Then write each one on the correct diagram.

1.

2.

3.

4.

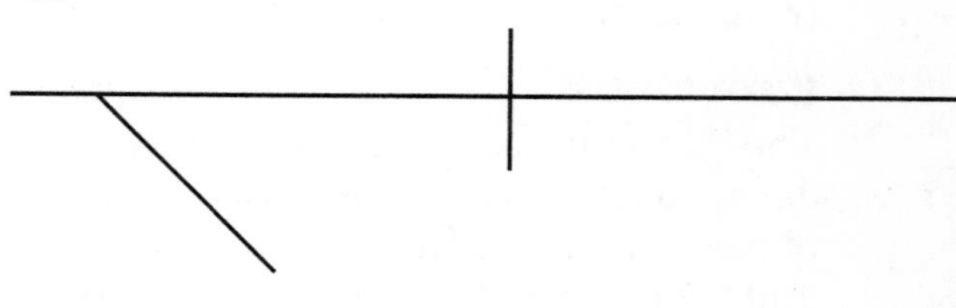

5.

EXERCISE 3

Name______________________________

Unscramble the following groups of words to make complete sentences and then diagram.

1. talk politicians ____
2. advertise companies ____________________________________
3. serve waiters the ______________________________________
4. stinks garbage ____
5. chill refrigerators _____________________________________

EXERCISE 4

Find the mistakes in the following diagrams. Then, diagram the sentences correctly.

1. Tigers roar.

Tigers roar

2. Swallows will return.

Swallows | return will

3. A gorilla gazes.

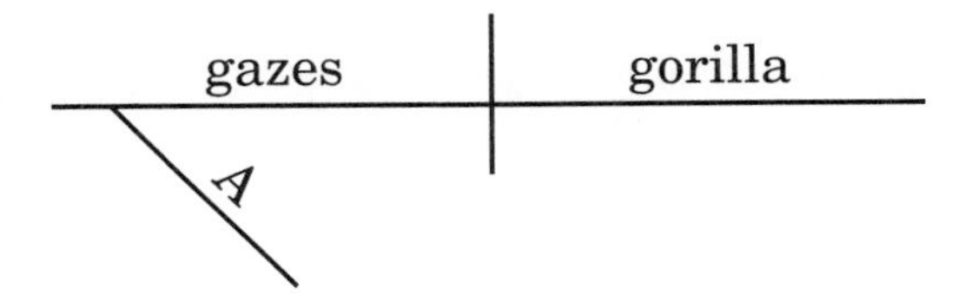

4. Elephants amble.

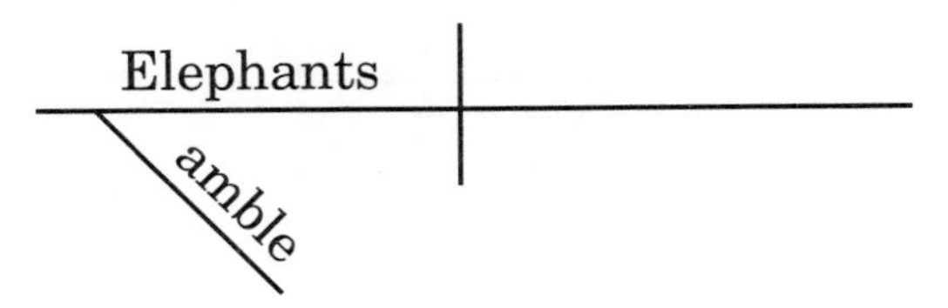

5. The mosquitoes bite.

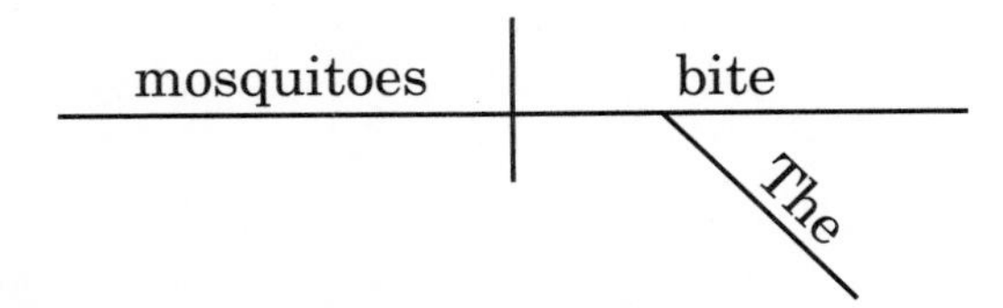

Compound Subjects

Name________________________________

Sentences that contain compound subjects require two parallel lines joined by diagonal lines to the horizontal line containing the verb. Notice how the conjunction is written on a dotted line connecting the subjects.

Examples:

Alison and Amanda won.

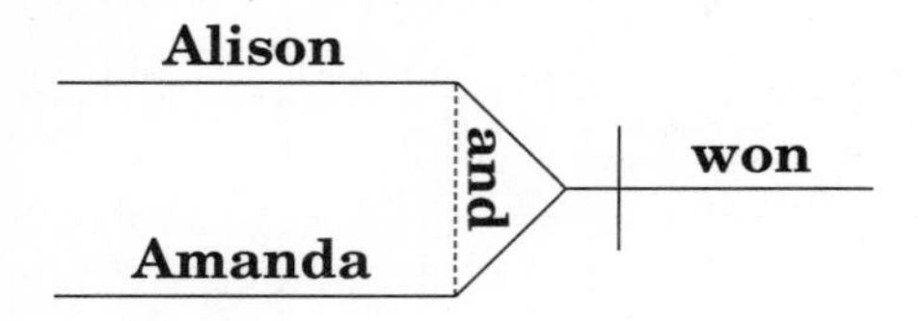

Tim and Tom wept.

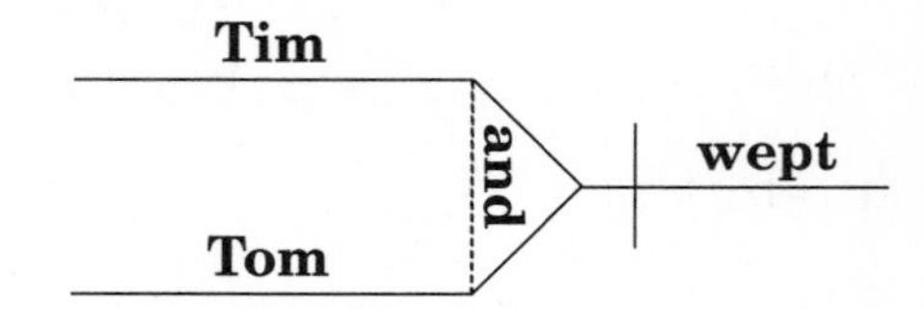

EXERCISE 1

In the following sentences, underline the subjects once and the verbs twice. Then diagram the sentences.

1. The soldiers and the civilians fled.
2. The shells and grenades exploded.
3. A fighter and a bomber collided.
4. The sailors and the marines fought.
5. The battle and the war were lost.
6. The horse and rider fell.
7. The castle and the parapet were taken.
8. General Grant and General Lee met.
9. The general and the officers surrendered.
10. The village and the countryside were destroyed.

EXERCISE 2

Create sentences to fit these diagrams. Then write each one on the correct diagram.

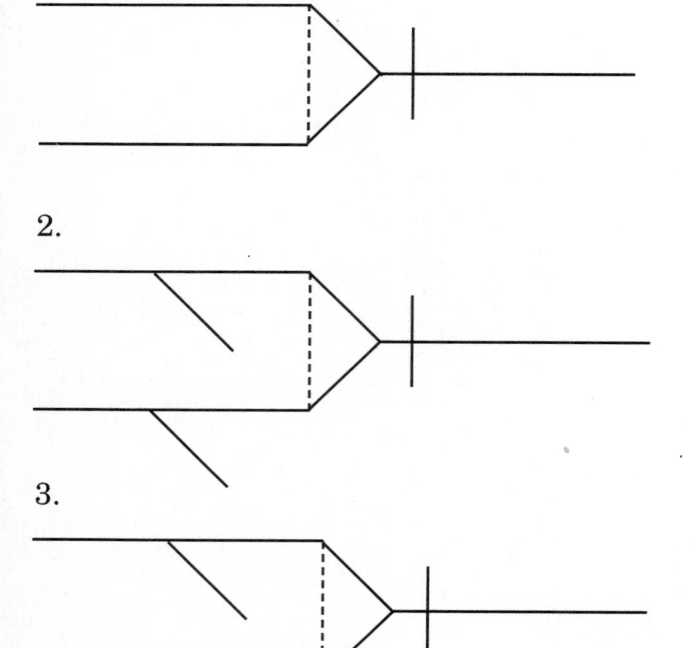

4.

5.

EXERCISE 3 **Name**____________________

Unscramble the following groups of words to make complete sentences and then diagram.

1. climbed Jack Ray and ____________________
2. were the basketball and football the leaking ____________________
____
3. aunt visited and uncle my ____________________
4. passed and trucks cars ____________________
5. fell meteors asteroids and ____________________

EXERCISE 4

Find the mistakes in the following diagrams. Then, on a sheet of paper, diagram the sentences correctly.

1. The cavalry and the infantry retreated.

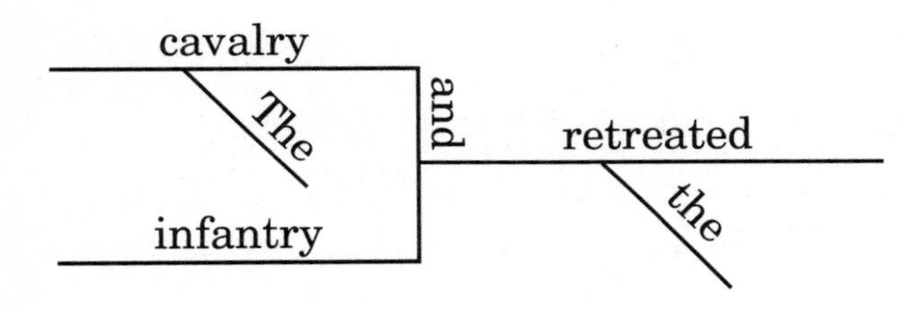

2. Decency and honor must prevail.

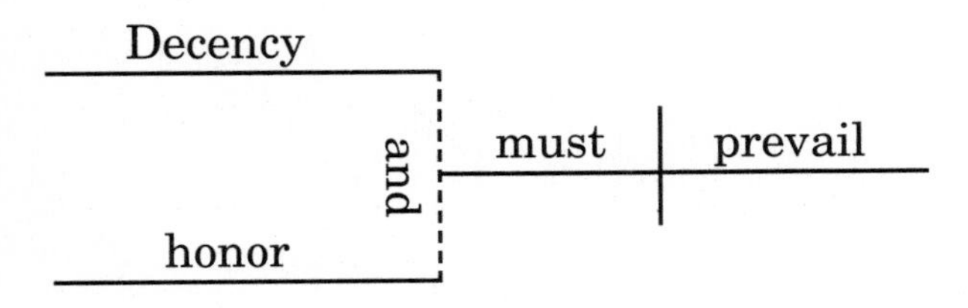

3. Cannons and shells were moved.

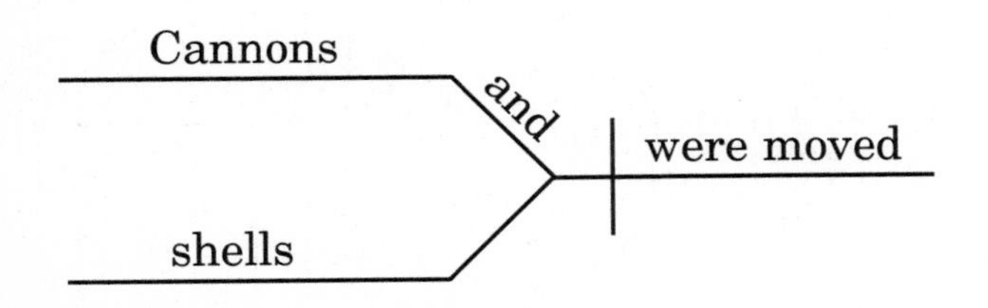

4. The swords and the daggers were melted.

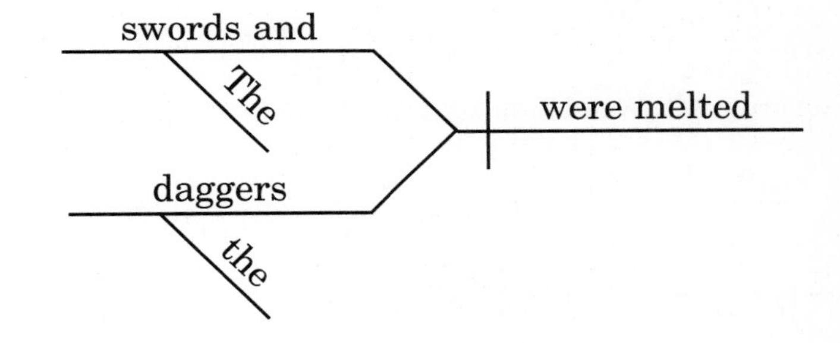

5. Peace and contentment are coming.

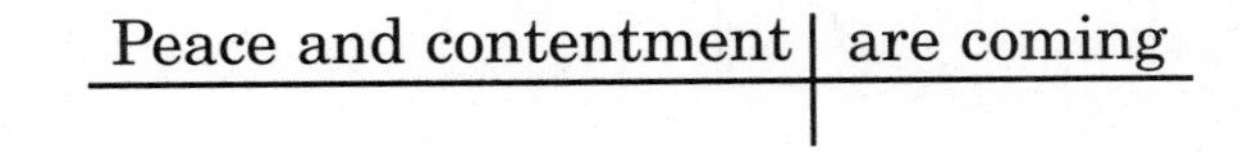

Compound Verbs

Name______________________________

Sentences that contain compound verbs require two parallel lines joined by diagonal lines to the horizontal line containing the subject. Notice how the conjunction(s) is/are written on a dotted line connecting the verbs.

Examples:

Blaine came and left.

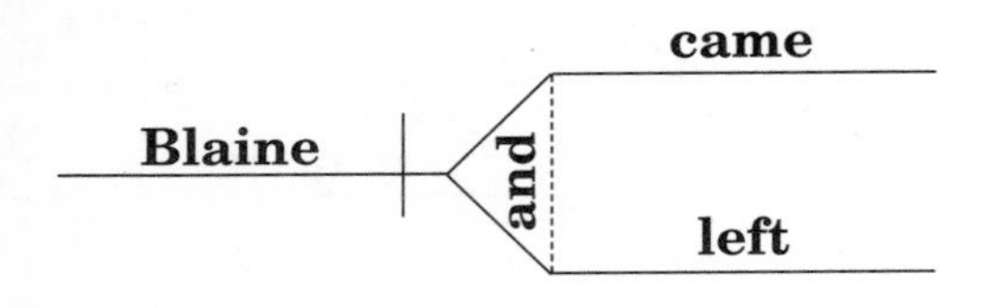

The audience will either cheer or boo.

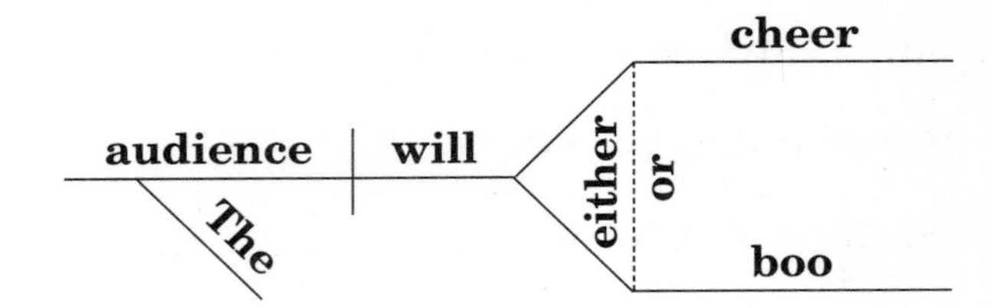

EXERCISE 1

In the following sentences, underline the subjects once and the verbs twice. Then diagram the sentences.

1. She swung and missed.
2. Kenisha and Reva ate and drank.
3. Frederick either plays or watches.
4. The lioness prowled or slept.
5. The hen and the rooster watched and waited.
6. John and Gwen will listen and decide.
7. The crowd clapped and cheered.
8. The nomads packed and fled.
9. A dog can growl and whimper.
10. The Japanese and the Americans met and agreed.

EXERCISE 2

Create sentences to fit these diagrams. Then write each one on the correct diagram.

1.

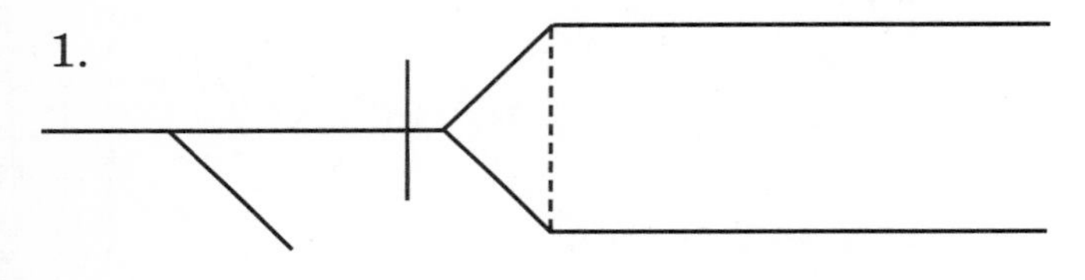

2.

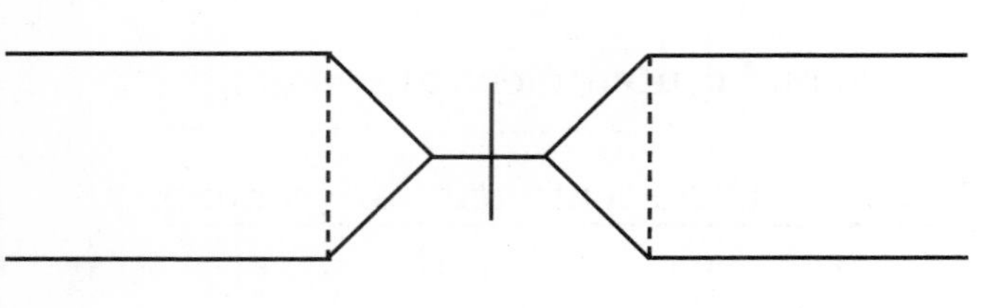

3.

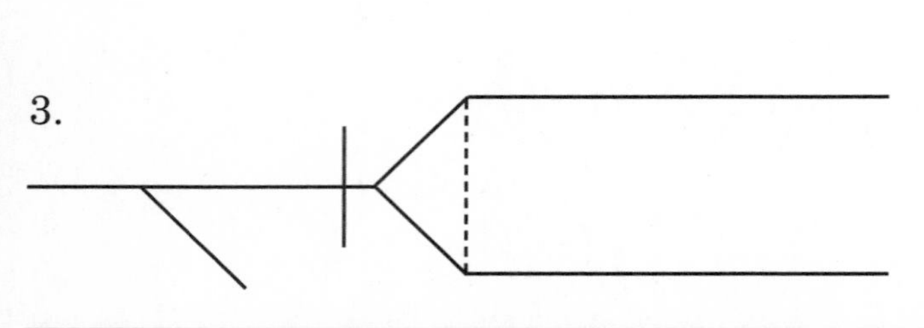

4.

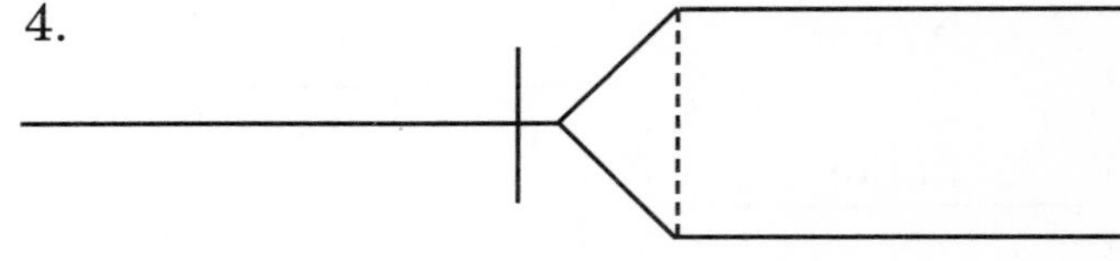

5.

EXERCISE 3

Name________________________

Unscramble the following groups of words to make complete sentences and then diagram.

1. screamed yelled and the coach______________________________
2. and fired soldiers ran the ______________________________
3. sat students listened teachers the and the and______________________________
4. stumbled calf the and fell ______________________________
5. picketed cancelled was rodeo and the ______________________________

EXERCISE 4

Find the mistakes in the following diagrams. Then, on a sheet of paper, diagram the sentences correctly.

1. Nobody can talk and listen.

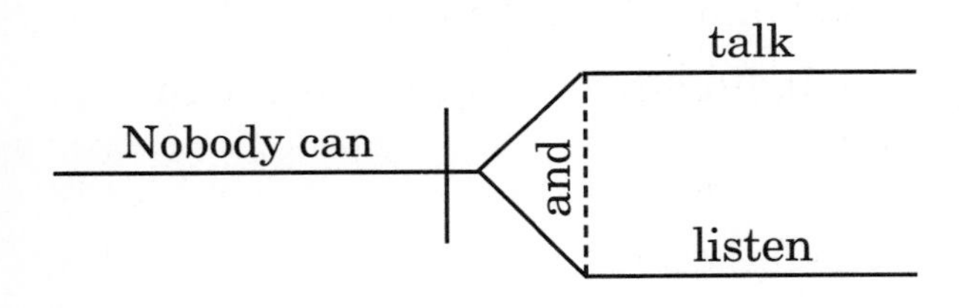

2. The rabbi chanted and sang.

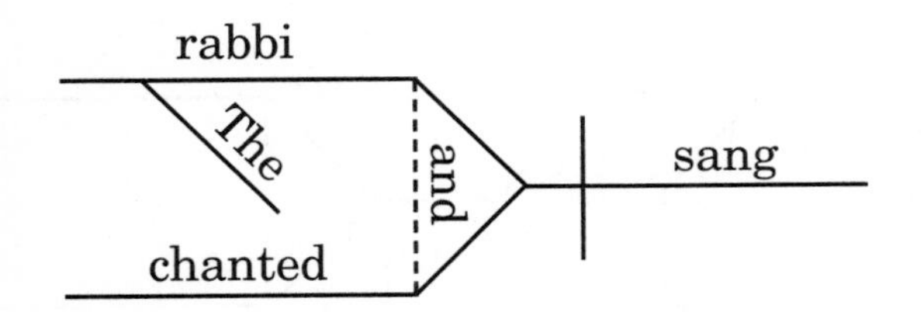

3. The French and the English disagreed and fought.

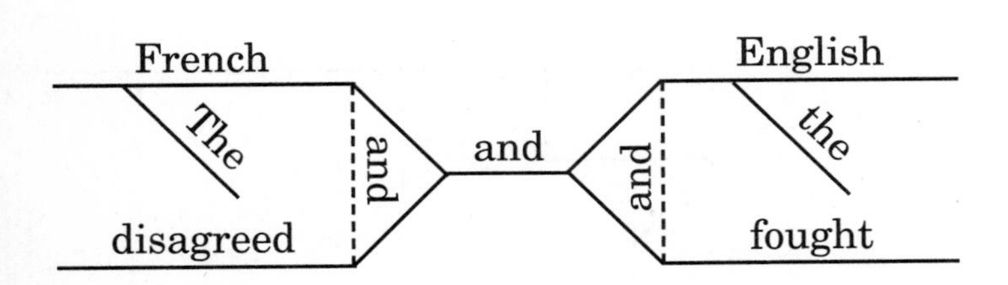

4. A mother and child cuddled and slept.

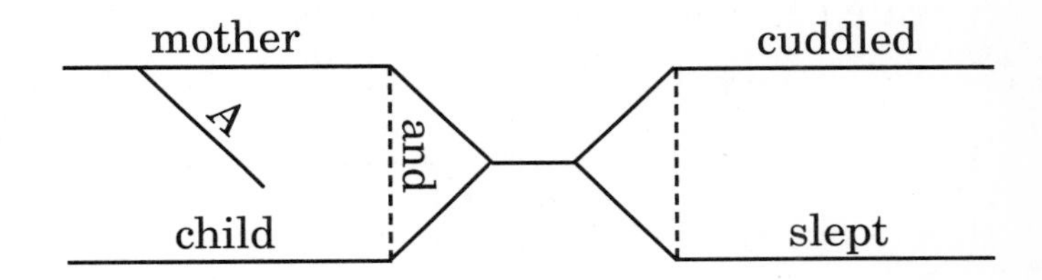

5. The computer flickered and flashed.

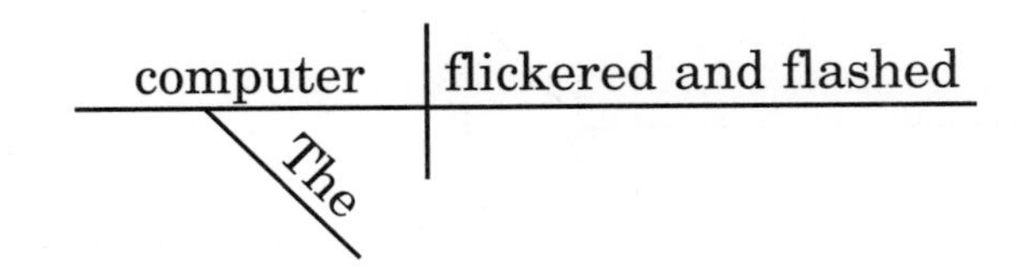

Adjective Modifiers

Name_______________________________

An adjective is placed on a slanted line beneath the noun that it modifies.

Examples:

The red fish swam.

fish | swam

The red

A blue dolphin leapt and splashed.

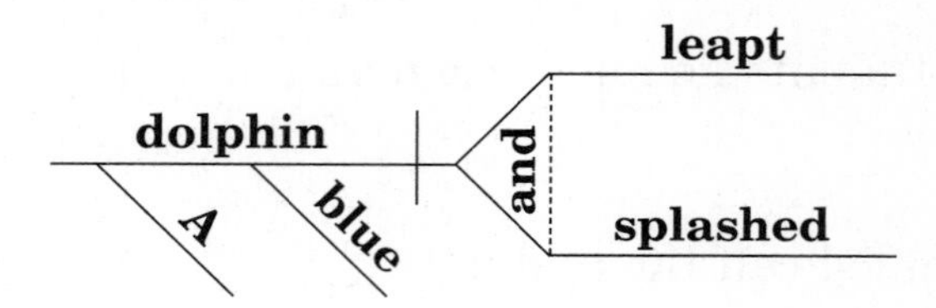

EXERCISE 1

In the following sentences, underline the adjectives and then diagram the sentences.

1. A big ship will roll.
2. Blue-green water boiled and seethed.
3. Light, fluffy clouds skittered and raced.
4. A crusty crab scuttled.
5. A cool drink would help.
6. Huge waves crashed.
7. The hot sand hurt.
8. The fair-skinned people burned.
9. A red umbrella collapsed.
10. The lighted pier and the dark night clashed.

EXERCISE 2

Create sentences to fit these diagrams. Then write each one on the correct diagram.

1.

2.

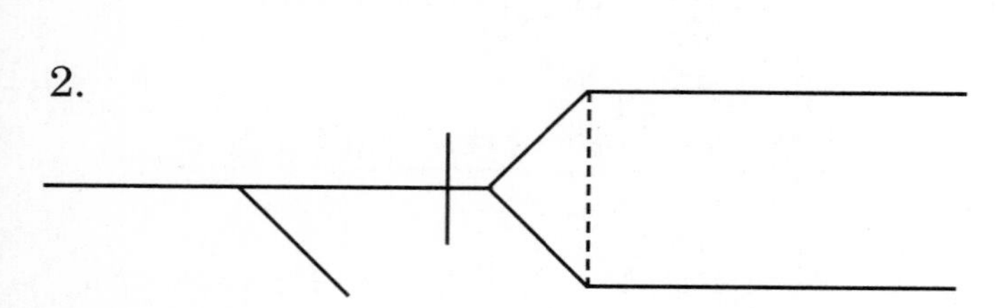

3.

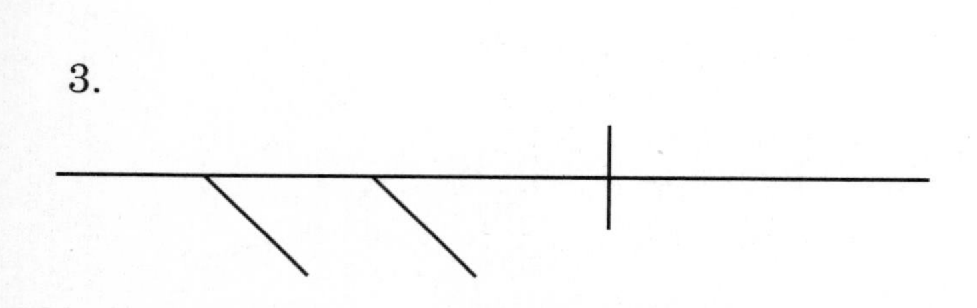

4.

5.

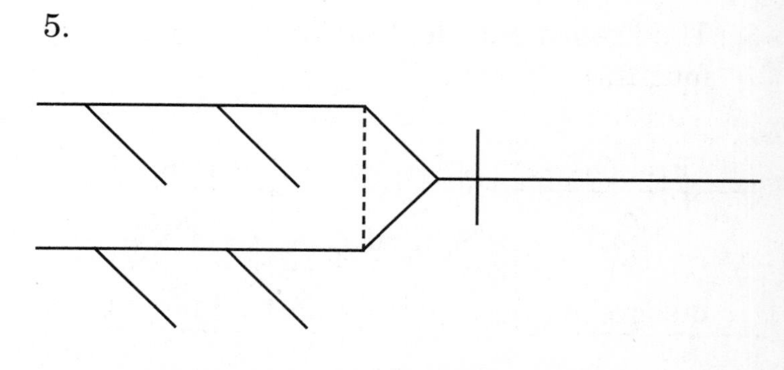

EXERCISE 3 **Name**________________________

Unscramble the following groups of words to make complete sentences and then diagram.

1. crushed the were roses red ________________________________
2. violets purple the bloomed ________________________________
3. flashy will race new car the silver ____________________________
4. spoiled the cried boy little________________________________
5. charged bull the raging __________________________________

EXERCISE 4

Find the mistakes in the following diagrams. Then, on a sheet of paper, diagram the sentences correctly.

1. A glass fish tank can break.

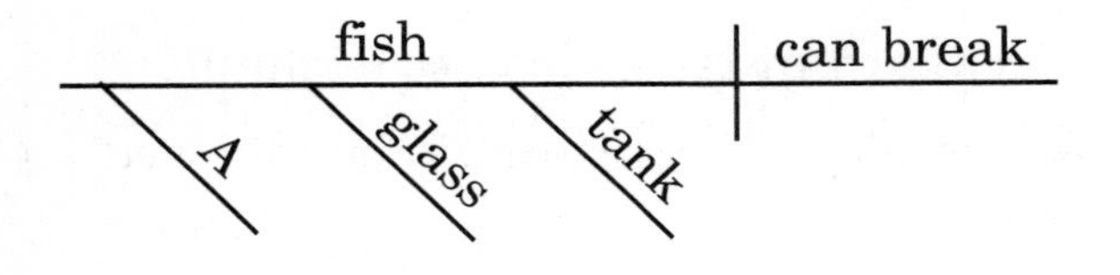

2. The big blue kite soared.

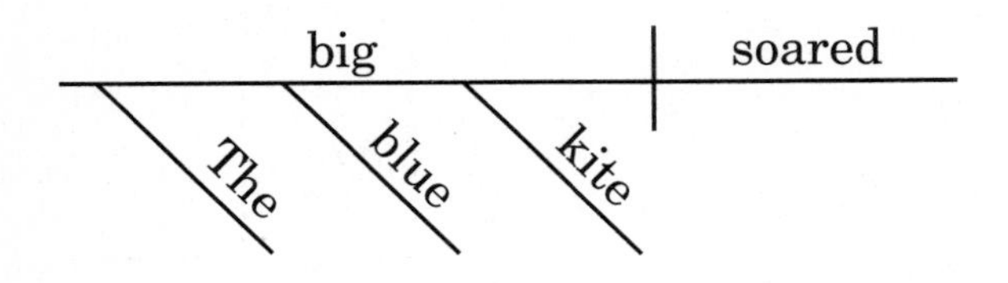

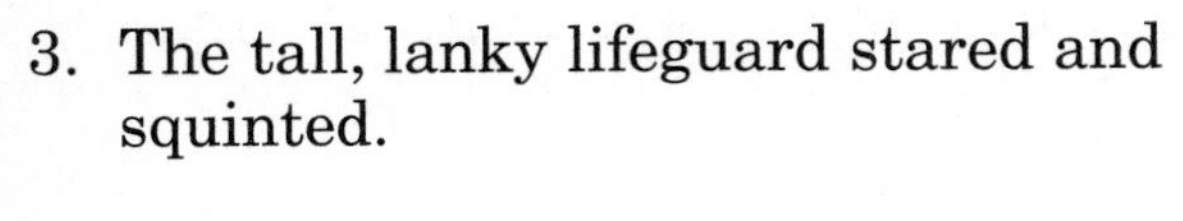

3. The tall, lanky lifeguard stared and squinted.

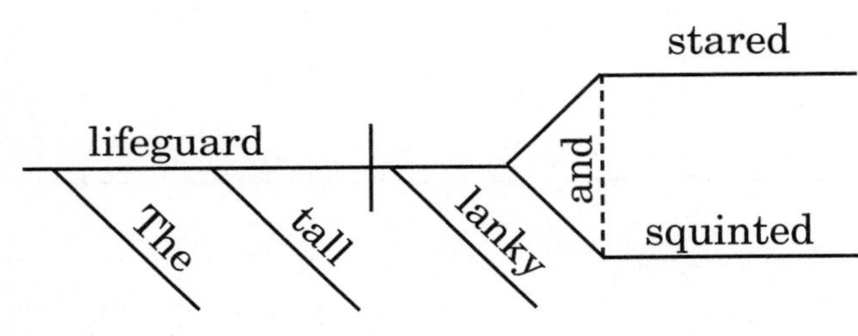

4. Many young people can swim.

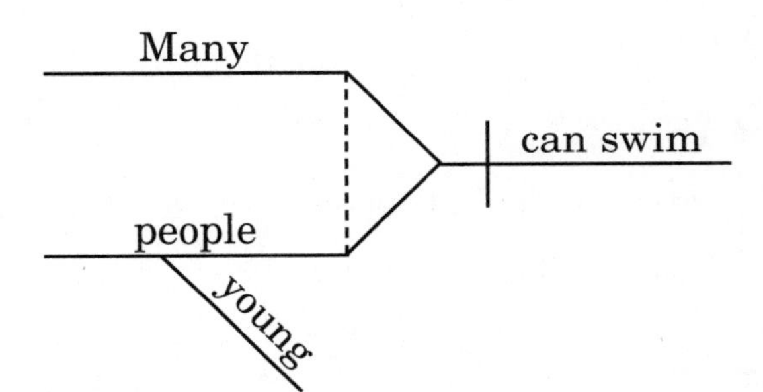

5. The tin pail and the plastic shovel disappeared.

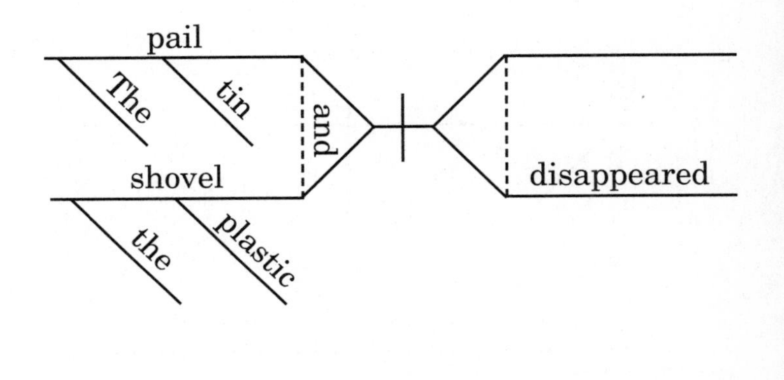

Adverb Modifiers

Name______________________________

An adverb is placed on a slanted line beneath the verb it modifies. An adverb that modifies an adjective or another adverb is placed on a line parallel to the word it modifies and connected to it by a slanted line.

Examples:

Cold and miserable weather often occurs here.

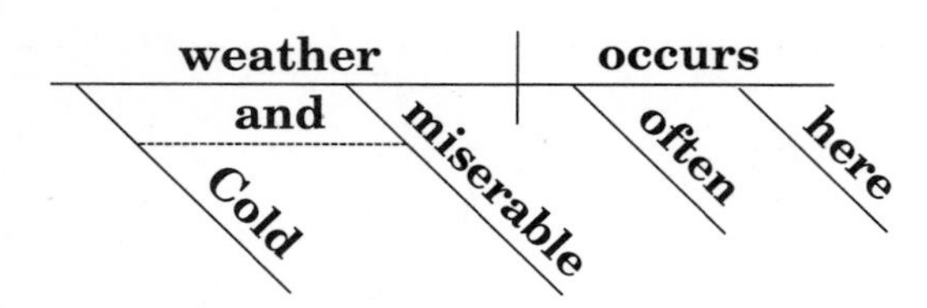

The flashy car drove past very quickly.

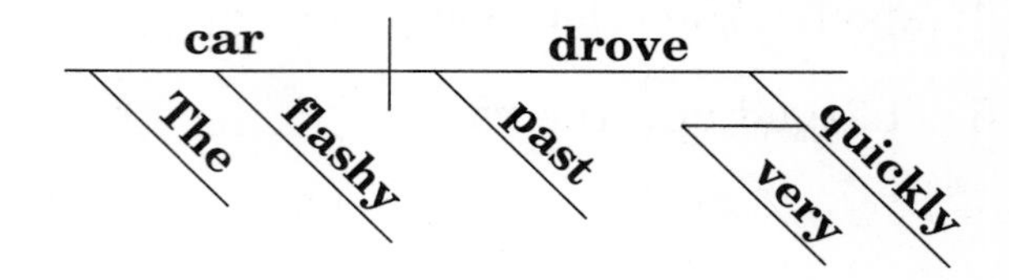

EXERCISE 1

In the following sentences, underline the adverbs and then diagram the sentences.

1. The gas flame burned brightly.
2. The wheat bread had been baked too long.
3. Sally and Rachel cleaned all night.
4. Raul and Jason always cooperated.
5. The antiquated refrigerator always ran noisily.
6. Good cooks saute and simmer slowly.
7. Certain fish dishes must be served carefully.
8. Hot spices should be used sparingly.
9. A restaurant is needed occasionally.
10. A complicated recipe must be followed exactly.

EXERCISE 2

Create sentences to fit these diagrams. Then write each one on the correct diagram.

1.

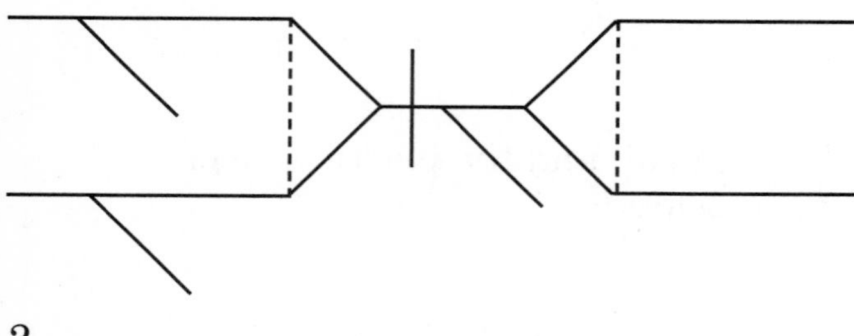

2.

3.

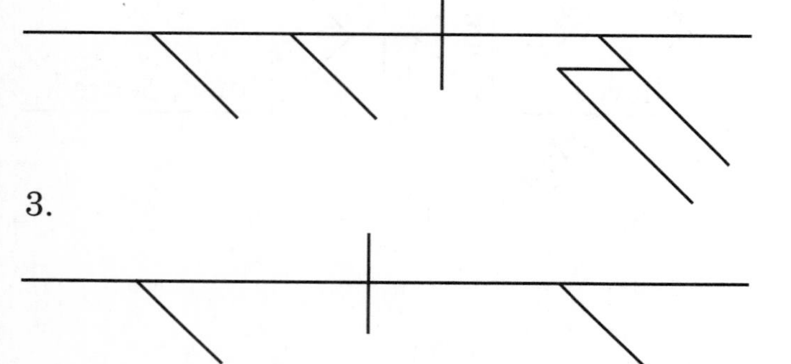

4.

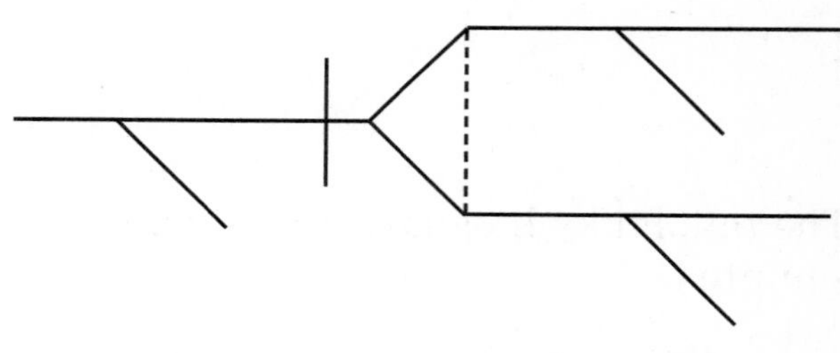

5.

EXERCISE 3

Name________________________________

Unscramble the following groups of words to make complete sentences and then diagram.

1. yesterday prisoners the escaped ____
2. refugees the immediately returned were____________________________________

   ____

3. costs health rose higher ____
4. tonight play team the will ____

   ____

5. served ball the was wide ____

EXERCISE 4

Find the mistakes in the following diagrams. Then, on a sheet of paper, diagram the sentences correctly.

1. Calvin skated lightly.

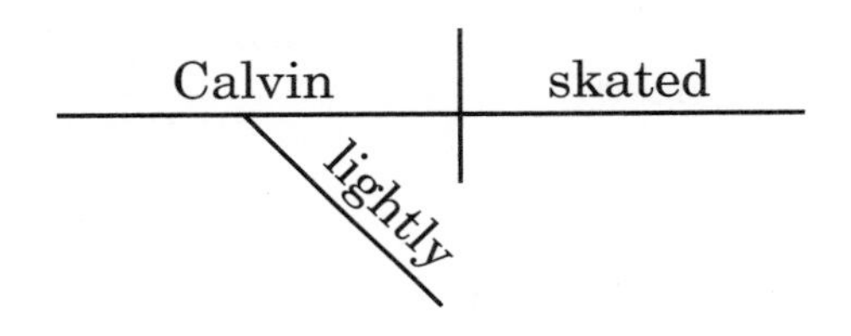

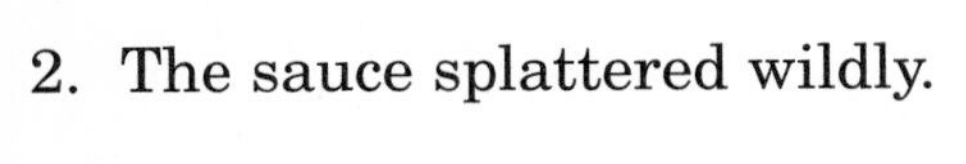

2. The sauce splattered wildly.

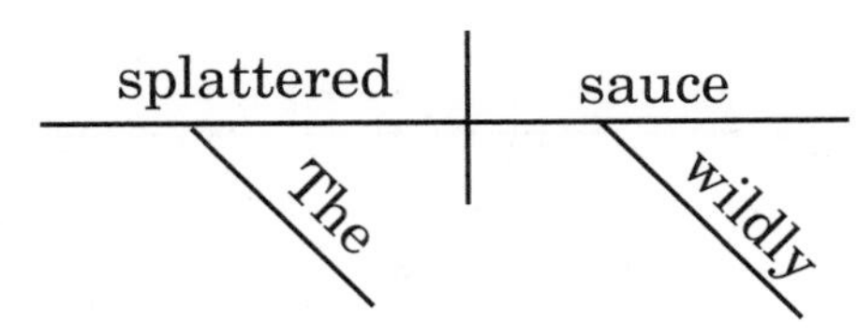

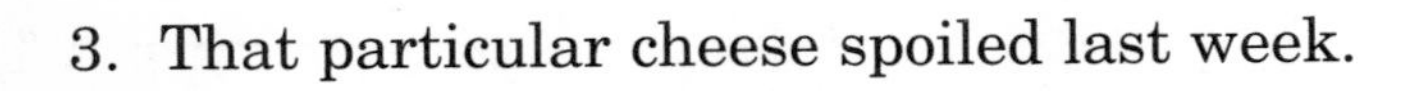

3. That particular cheese spoiled last week.

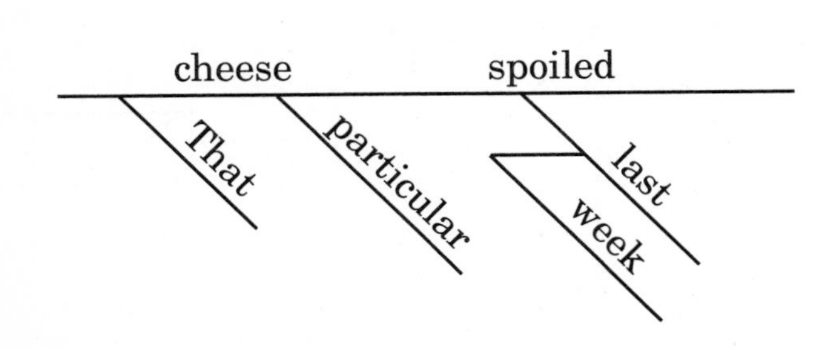

4. The pan and its lid clanged very noisily.

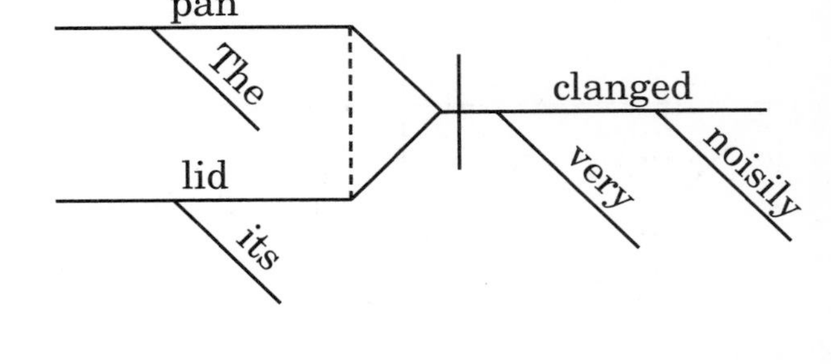

5. The gasoline container exploded forcefully.

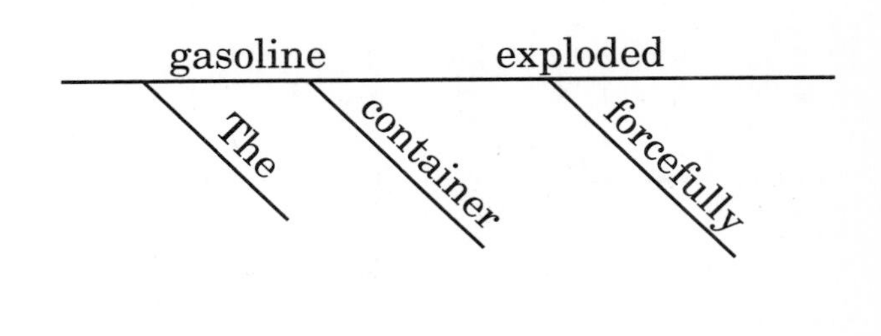

Appositives

Name____________________________

An appositive is placed in parentheses following the word it identifies or explains. Any words which modify the appositive should be placed on slanted lines directly beneath it.

Examples:

Mr. Poon, our English teacher, won easily.

Mr. Poon **(teacher)** | **won**
our **English** **easily**

Venice, a famous Italian city, was conquered that year.

Venice **(city)** | **was conquered**
a **famous** **Italian** **year** **that**

EXERCISE 1

In the following sentences, underline the appositives once and their modifiers twice. Then diagram the sentences.

1. Kerri, my older sister, left immediately.
2. His car, a vintage roadster, crashed.
3. The senator, a Democrat, voted today.
4. That man, the village chief, will command.
5. Baseball, my favorite sport, ended yesterday.
6. His house, a rambling dump, burned down.
7. The dog, a huge shepherd, jumped up.
8. The boat, a sleek cruiser, slid past.
9. My cat, a grey manx, stretched and yawned.
10. Mr. Tobias, our Latin teacher, stood up and shouted.

EXERCISE 2

Create sentences to fit these diagrams. Then write each one on the correct diagram.

1.

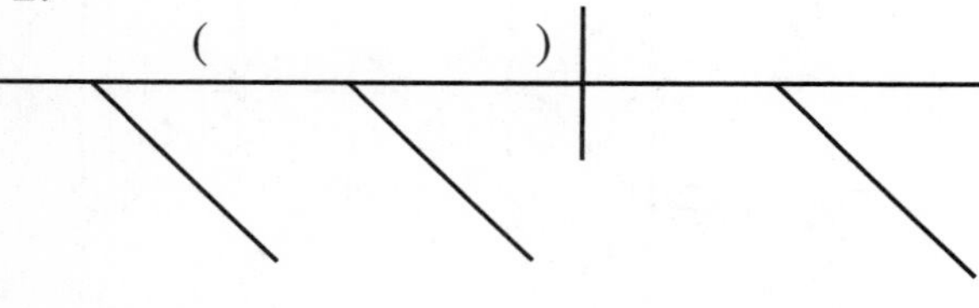

2.

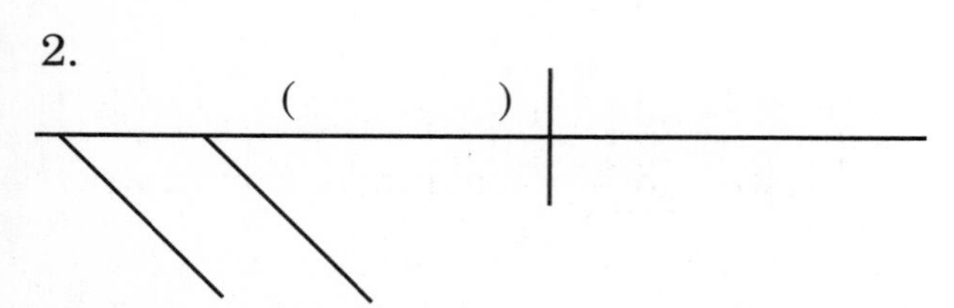

3.

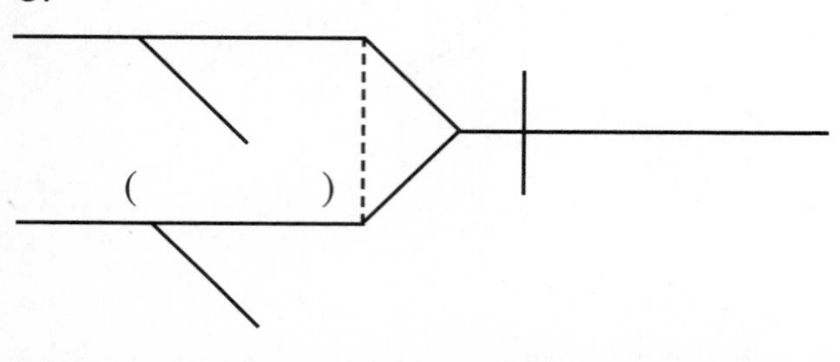

4.

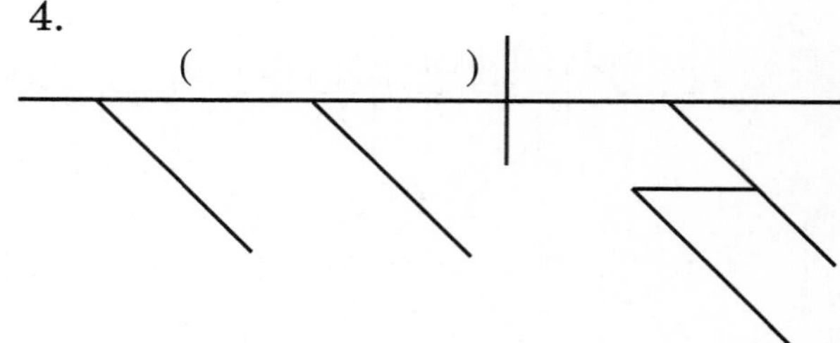

5.

( )

EXERCISE 3

Name______________________________

Unscramble the following groups of words to make complete sentences and then diagram.

1. my friend best Fidel moving is ______________________________
2. catcher is their batting best player the next ______________________________

   ____
3. real Batman jumped a crime fighter down ______________________________
4. especially an large spider tarantula disappeared the ______________________________

   ____
5. all "A" Horace student an won ______________________________

EXERCISE 4

Find the mistakes in the following diagrams. Then, on a sheet of paper, diagram the sentences correctly.

1. Terri Travis, the chairman, officiated.

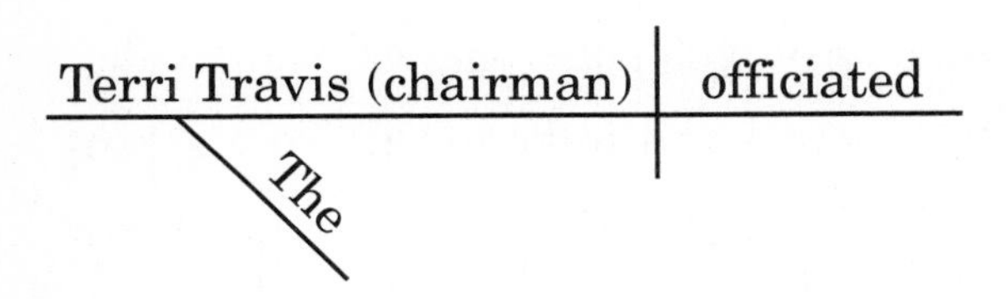

2. Tiko Tanaka, our mailman, passed by.

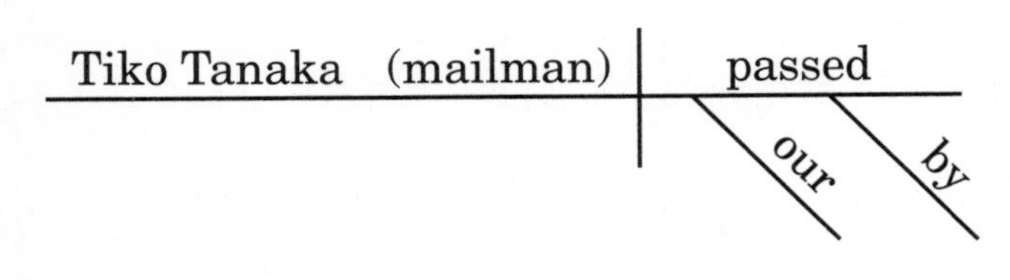

3. My dog, the runt, was pushed down.

dog (runt) | was pushed

down

4. The new girl, a very good student, will graduate tomorrow.

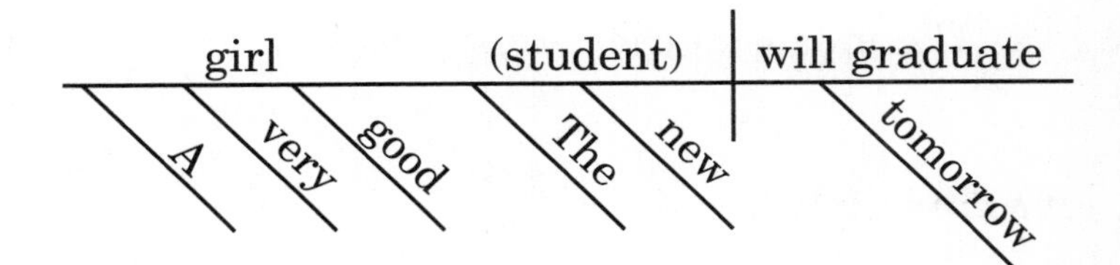

5. Stubby McKenzie, the fastest player, will lead.

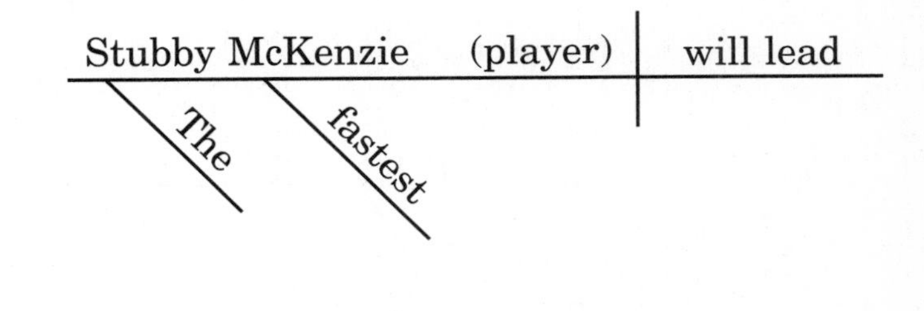

Adjective Prepositional Phrases

Name____________________________________

Adjective prepositional phrases are placed beneath the noun that they modify. The preposition is placed on a slanted line and its object is placed on a horizontal line connected to it. Modifiers of the object of the preposition are placed on slanted lines beneath the object.

Examples:

The puppy in the shop window jumped up.

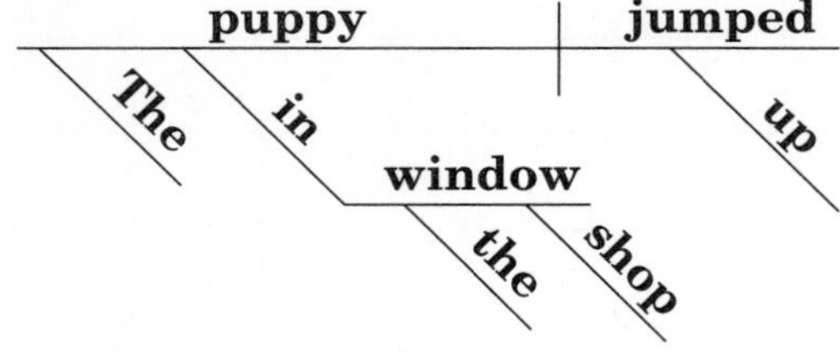

The novel by Hemingway was finally located.

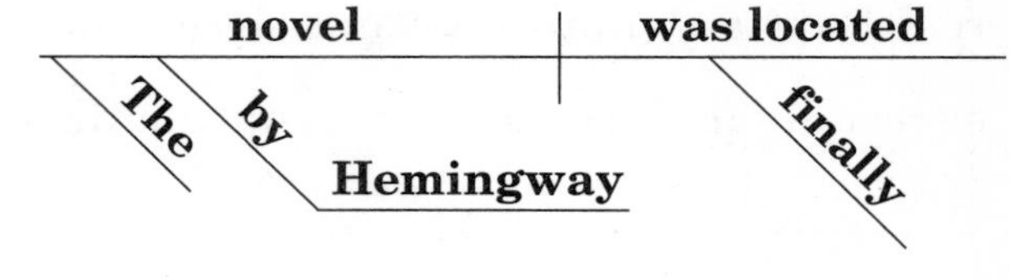

EXERCISE 1

In the following sentences, underline the prepositions once and their objects twice. Then diagram the sentences.

1. My friend with the broken arm is leaving.
2. The drugstore in town burned last night.
3. The musical with the best choreography will win.
4. A gorilla in a red jumpsuit and a chimpanzee in a chiffon dress ran away.
5. The music on the radio is disrupting.
6. The list of students' addresses was accidentally burned.
7. Nobody in this class knows.
8. The doctors in the hospital are working very hard.
9. The combination to the safe is lost.
10. The cottage beside the brook was sold yesterday.

EXERCISE 2

Create sentences to fit these diagrams. Then write each one on the correct diagram.

1.

2.

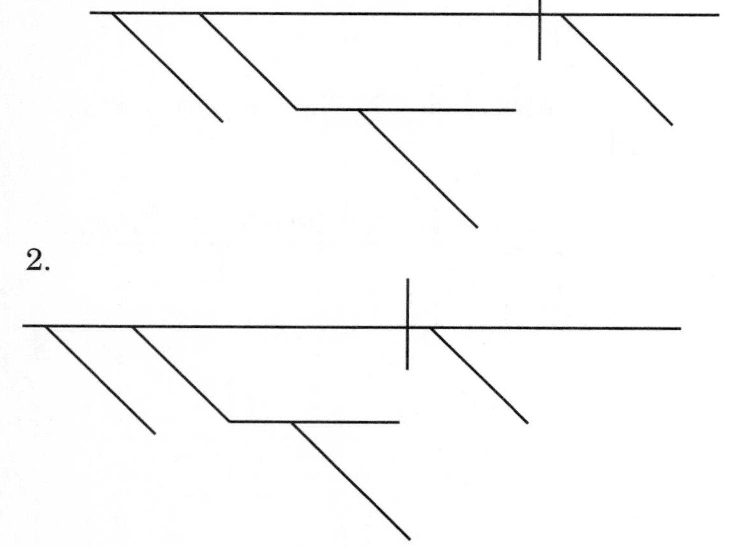

3.

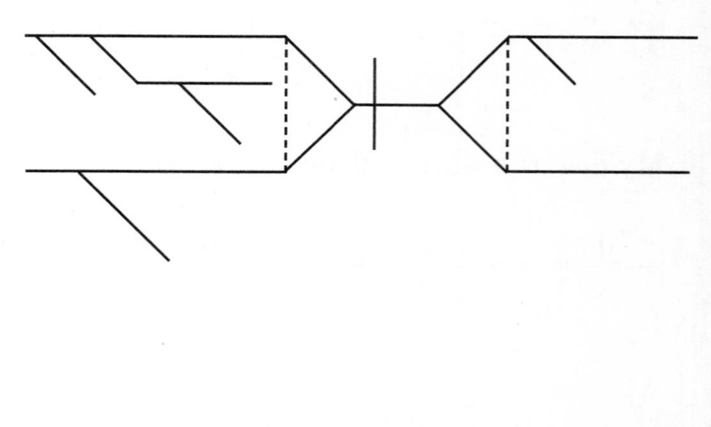

EXERCISE 3

Name____________________________________

Unscramble the following groups of words to make complete sentences and then diagram.

1. inside camera the used was bank the ____________________________________
2. house built quickly the on hill the was ____________________________________
3. first with flew equipment plane the the ____________________________________

   ____
4. hired with singer the was the voice golden____________________________________

   ____
5. cave fossils the disappeared in the ____________________________________

   ____

EXERCISE 4

Find the mistakes in the following diagrams. Then, on a sheet of paper, diagram the sentences correctly.

1. The time for business is now.

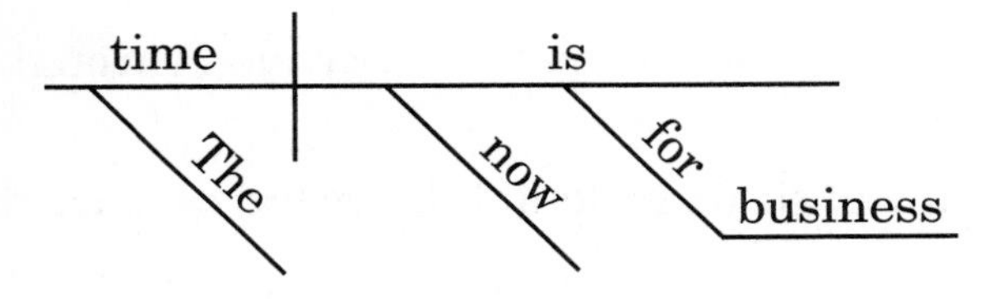

2. Matthew and Jason, friends to the end, returned today.

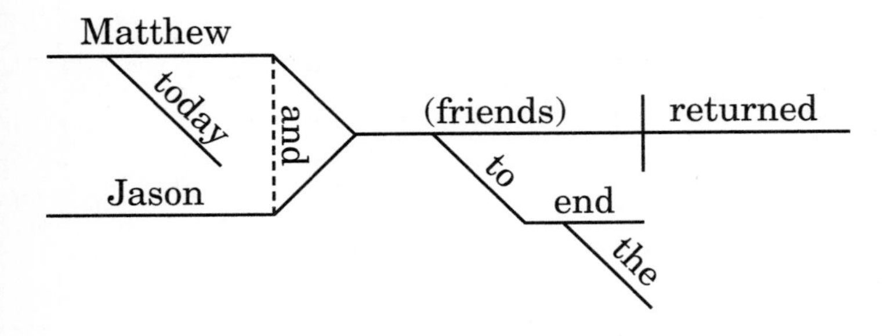

3. The wax on the floor glistened brightly.

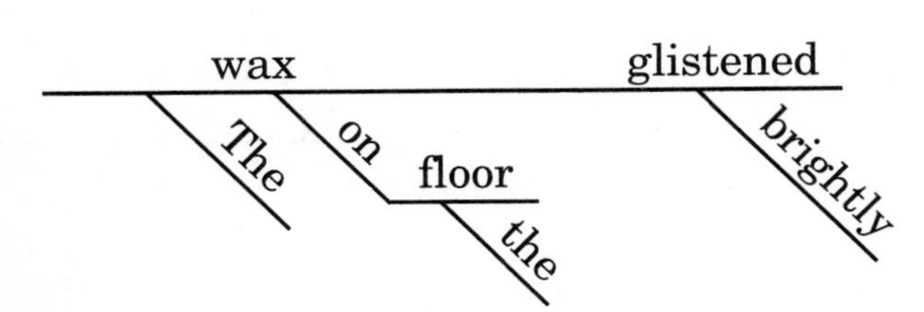

4. The table beside the desk collapsed.

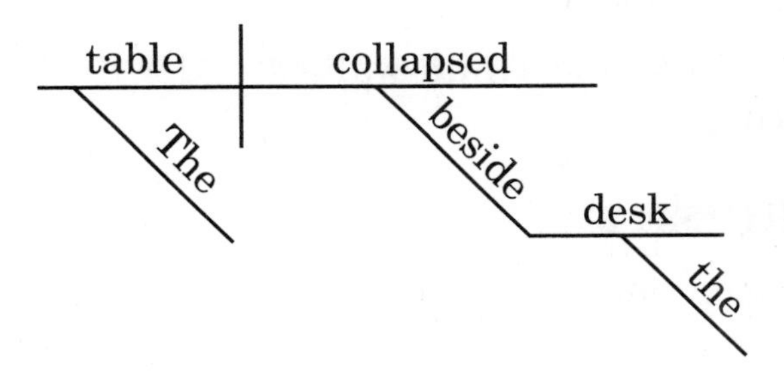

5. A magazine with lots of health hints will sell very well.

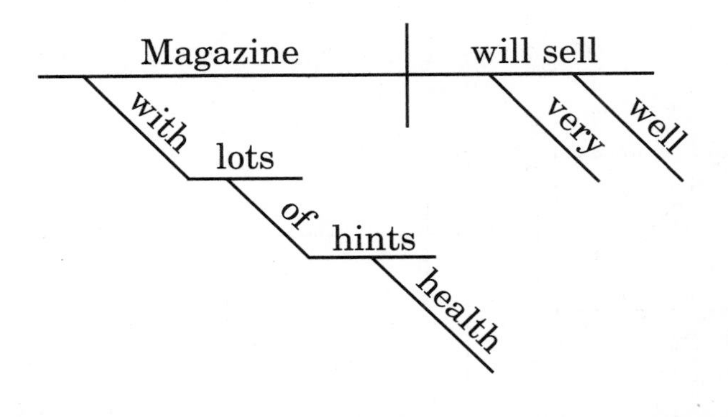

Adverb Prepositional Phrases

Name________________________________

Adverb prepositional phrases are placed beneath the verb, adjective, or other adverb that they modify. The preposition is placed on a slanted line, and the object of the preposition is placed on a horizontal line connected to it. Modifiers of the object of the preposition are placed on slanted lines beneath the object.

Examples:

The green car flew over the wall.

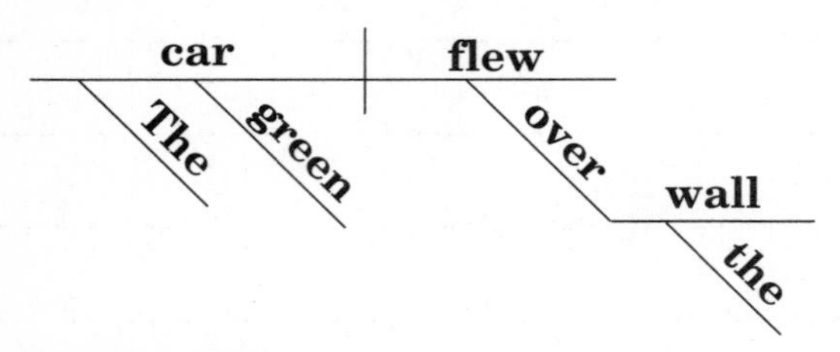

That park is across the wide, busy street.

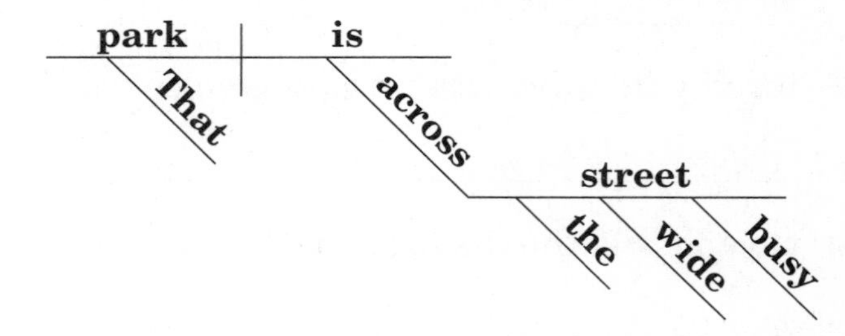

EXERCISE 1

In the following sentences, underline the prepositions once and the objects of the prepositions twice. Then diagram the sentences.

1. The bench sagged under the students' weight.
2. My biology book splashed into the water noisily.
3. Ron, the champion runner, jumped over the hurdle with ease.
4. The gifts were wrapped with care and placed under the tree.
5. Marithia and Tinita walked under the bridge.
6. Several jumpers were pushed from the plane too early.
7. The fire equipment was rushed into the forest.
8. After the defeat the team traveled through the night.
9. You will sit with Gerald under the barn eave.
10. The Amish travel everywhere in their buggies.

EXERCISE 2

Create sentences to fit these diagrams. Then write each one on the correct diagram.

1.

2.

3.

EXERCISE 3

Name________________________

Unscramble the following groups of words to make complete sentences and then diagram.

1. the bank in money is the ________________________
2. on his television new show is ________________________
3. the morning will we go in ________________________
4. music the concert energy with at in park the played was the ________________________

   ____
5. new during his last year purchased was computer the ________________________

   ____

EXERCISE 4

Find the mistakes in the following diagrams. Then, on a sheet of paper, diagram the sentences correctly.

1. Her cottage was located beside a quiet stream.

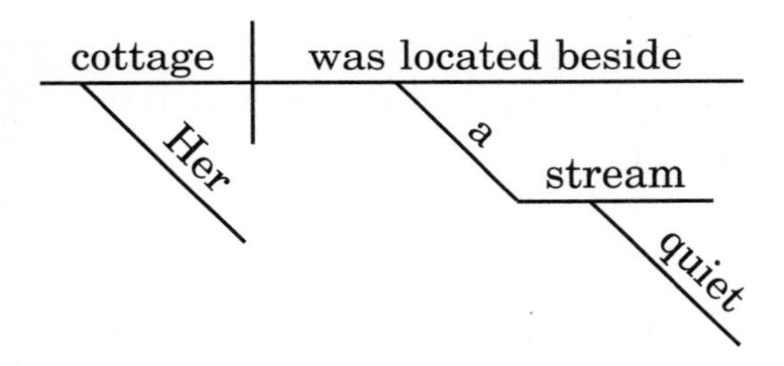

2. Monica laughed with delight.

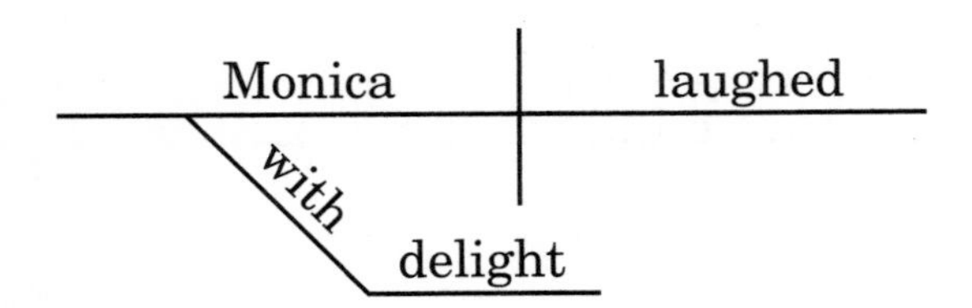

3. Nobody can know with certainty.

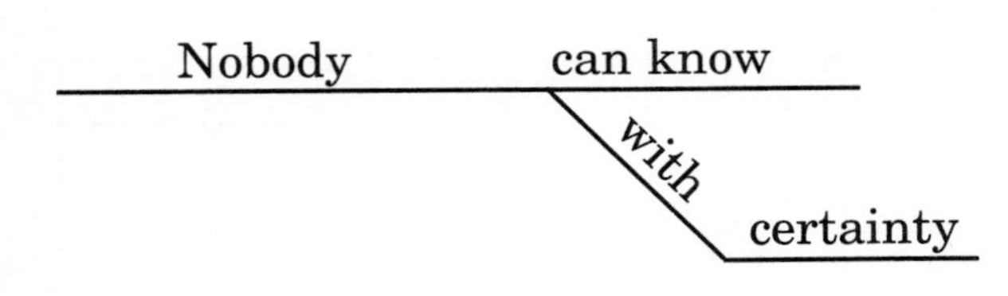

4. The set was designed by the art teacher.

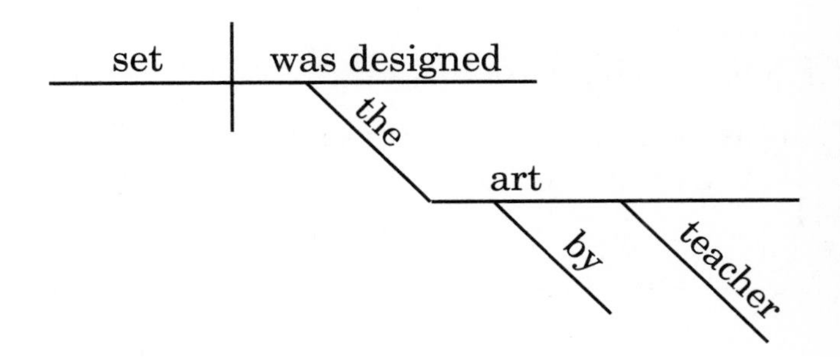

5 The minister and his Bible class left early in the morning.

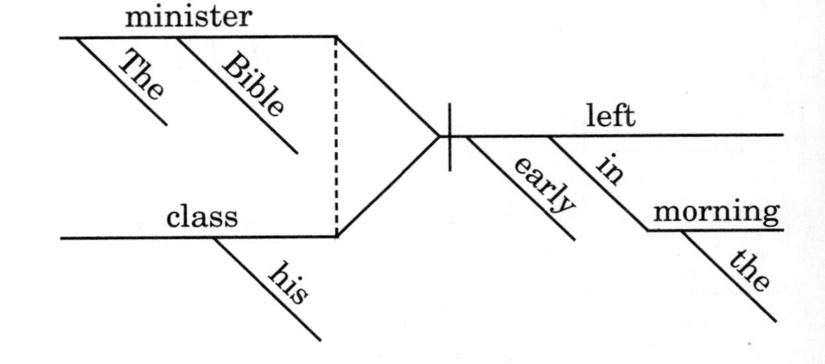

Subject Complements—Predicate Adjectives

Name____________________

A predicate adjective is placed on the same line as the subject and verb. It follows the linking verb and is separated from it by a line that slants back toward the subject it identifies or describes.

Examples:

This class is great.

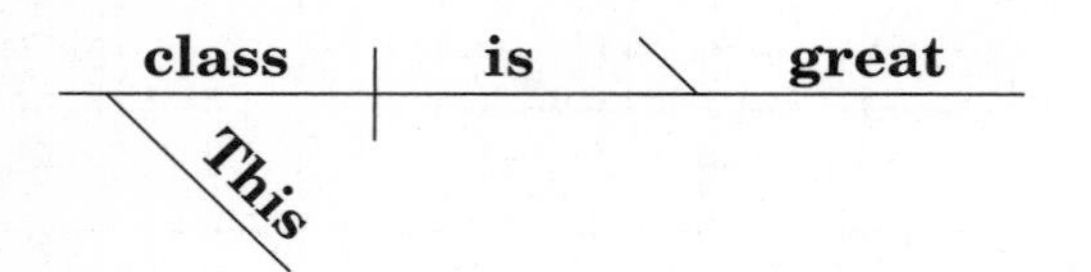

The roller coaster looks scary.

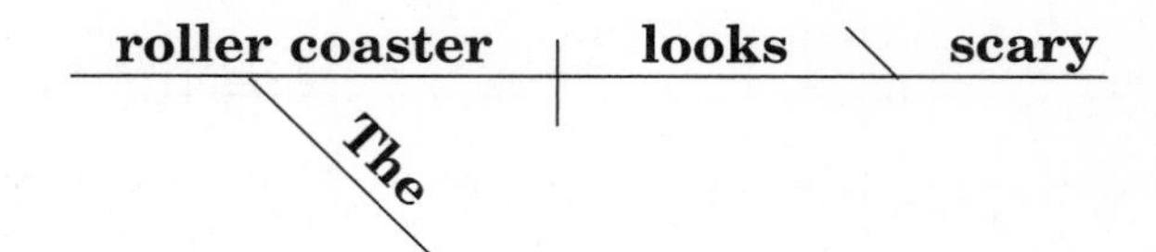

EXERCISE 1

In the following sentences, underline the predicate adjectives and then diagram the sentences.

1. Marcella appeared serene and content.
2. Reva became worried.
3. Henry felt ecstatic after the test.
4. The room remained silent after the fight.
5. This assignment is very hard.
6. The food in the cafeteria was terrible.
7. The men and women were happy with the results.
8. Summertime in Florida is usually hot.
9. The north parking lot was totally empty after the game.
10. Glenda and Trina seemed completely comfortable with me.

EXERCISE 2

Create sentences to fit these diagrams. Then write each one on the correct diagram.

1.

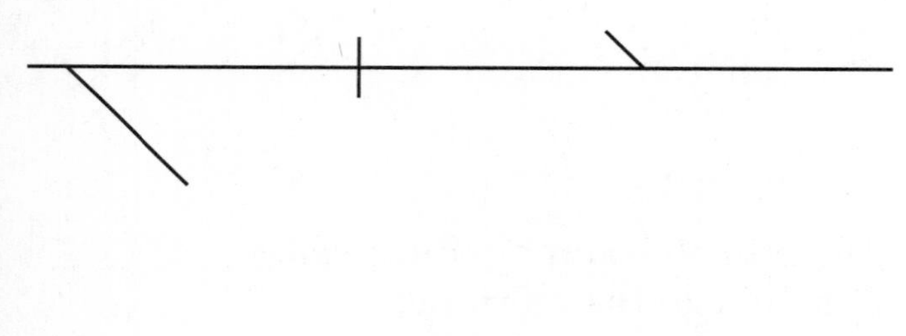

3.

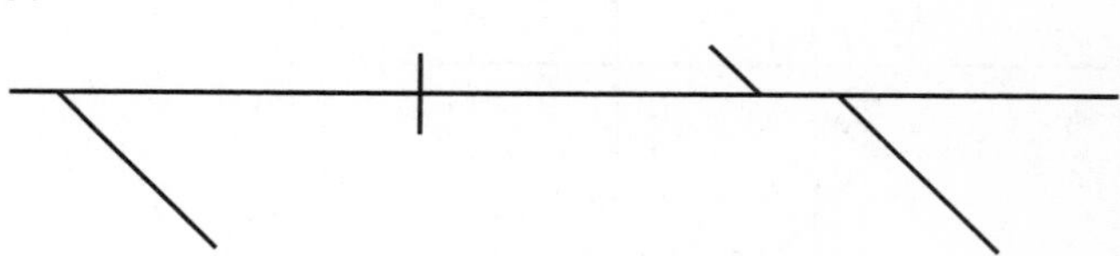

2.

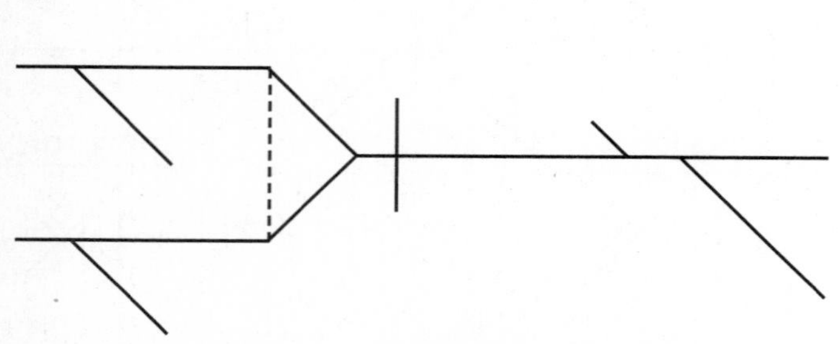

4.

EXERCISE 3 Name________________________

Unscramble the following groups of words to make complete sentences and then diagram.

1. horrifying wreck car was the ________________________
2. looked she marvelous ________________________
3. people loud were the stands the in ________________________
4. was teacher enthusiastic about Paul's work the ________________________
5. sick Doris became the night during ________________________

EXERCISE 4

Find the mistakes in the following diagrams. Then, on a sheet of paper, diagram the sentences correctly.

1. You should look calm for this scene.

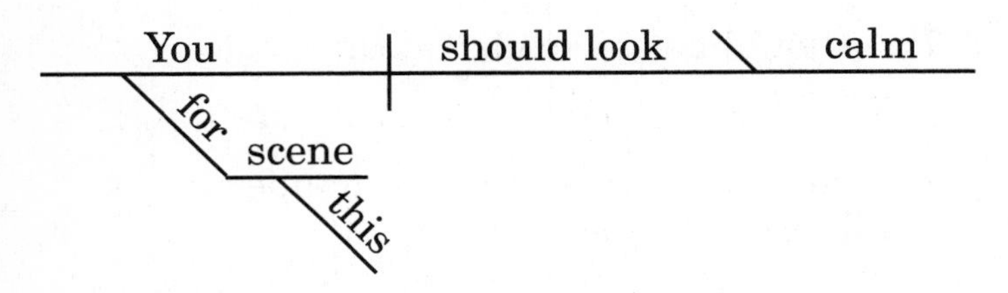

2. Frank and Elsie became lonely during the winter.

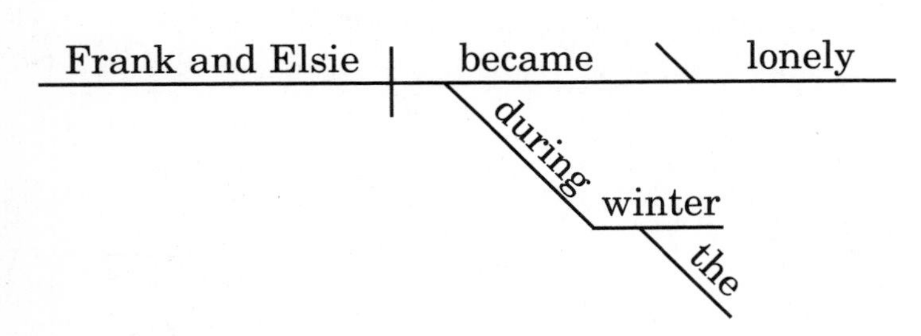

3. The cheese and the milk smell fresh.

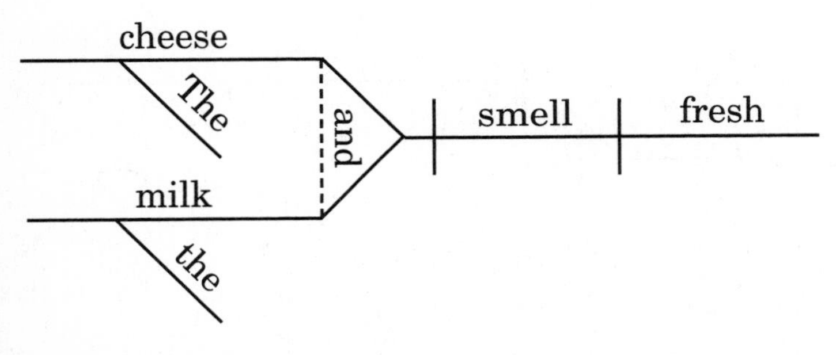

4. The plot became difficult and anticlimactic.

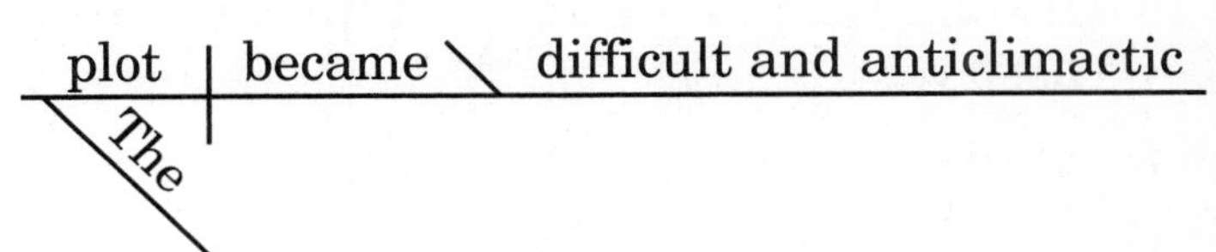

5. Tiffany is tallest and brightest in her family.

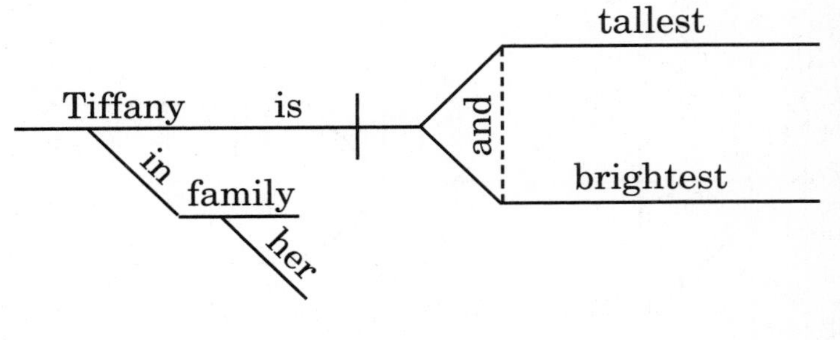

1-56822-175-4 *Diagraming*

Subject Complements—Predicate Nouns

Name__________________________________

A predicate nominative is placed on the same line as the subject and verb. It follows the linking verb and is separated from it by a line that slants back toward the subject it identifies or describes.

Examples:

Alonzo became a computer expert.

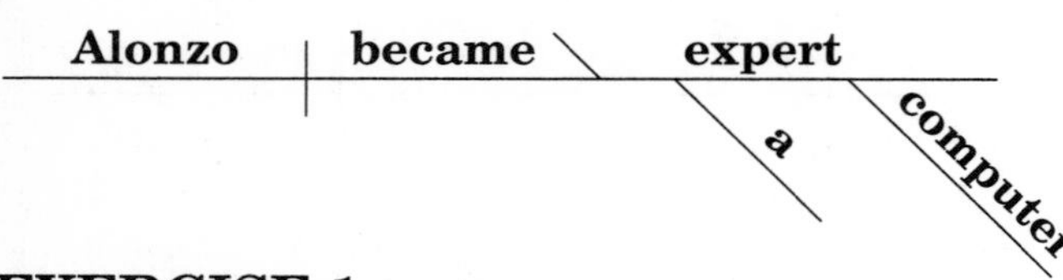

His biography was a best-seller.

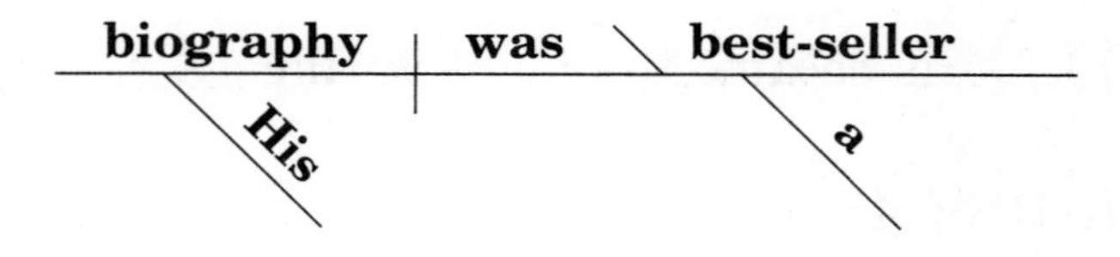

EXERCISE 1

In the following sentences, underline the predicate nouns and then diagram the sentences.

1. After his retirement Mark became a consultant.
2. Uncle Earl was the best storyteller in the family.
3. Ben is a talented student.
4. He will remain president of the club until next year.
5. St. Paul is the capital of Minnesota.
6. That is the most popular poem in the anthology.
7. I should be the leader of this group.
8. Mildred became an authority on fungi.
9. The President is the Commander in Chief.
10. Alaska became part of the United States in this century.

EXERCISE 2

Create sentences to fit these diagrams. Then write each one on the correct diagram.

1.

2.

3.

4.

5.

EXERCISE 3

Name______________________________

Unscramble the following groups of words to make complete sentences and then diagram.

1. some people to Malcolm X hero is a ______________________________
2. Mel with ball is man the the ______________________________
3. George that in story villain is the ______________________________
4. became overnight celebrities they ______________________________
5. pitcher great was Warren Spahn a ______________________________

EXERCISE 4

Find the mistakes in the following diagrams. Then, on a sheet of paper, diagram the sentences correctly.

1. My home is my castle.

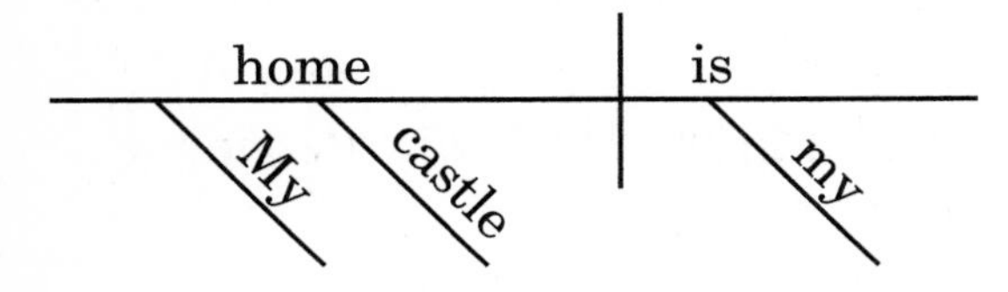

2. Michigan is my favorite state.

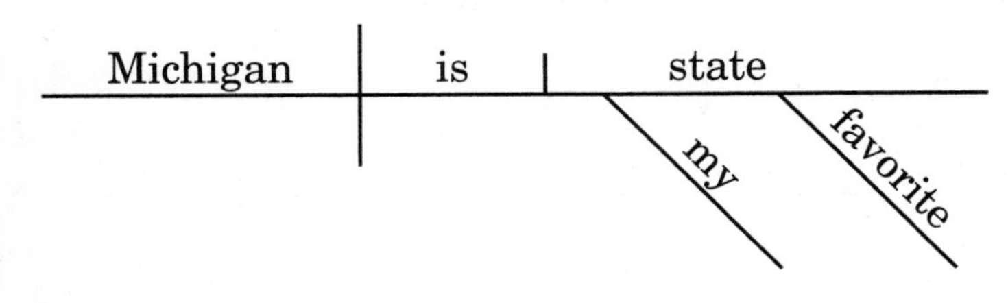

3. He was appointed treasurer.

He | was appointed

treasurer

4. The red-faced man is my uncle.

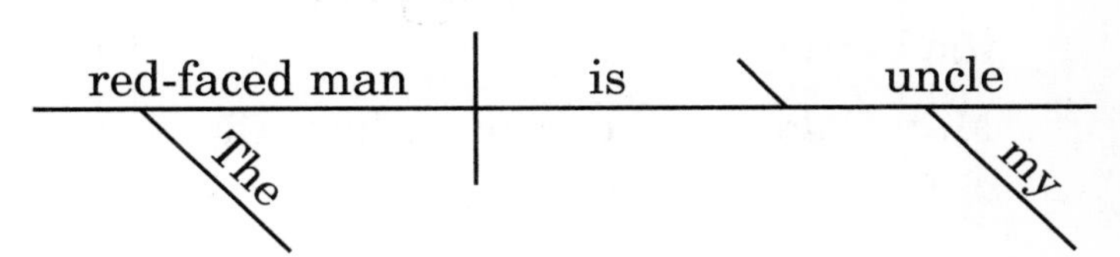

5. The girl with the ponytail is the class clown.

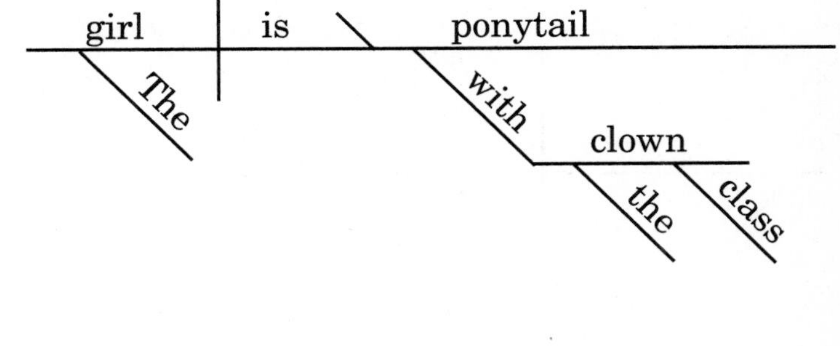

Direct Objects

Name______________________________

A direct object is placed on the same horizontal line as the subject and the verb. It is separated from the verb by a short vertical line which does not cross the horizontal line. Modifiers of the direct object are placed on slanted lines directly beneath it.

Examples:

The men tracked a bear.

The substitute teacher taught the class.

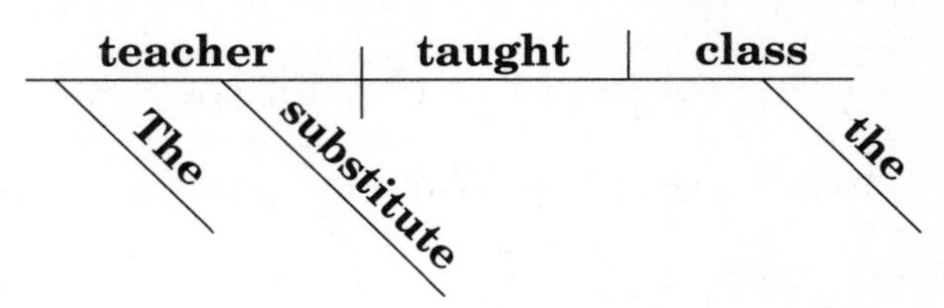

EXERCISE 1

In the following sentences, underline the verbs once and the direct objects twice. Then diagram the sentences.

1. The Polar Bears won the championship.
2. Darcy answered the teacher's question.
3. Without delay Jasper boarded the train.
4. The salesclerk in the men's department sold every pink shirt in stock.
5. President Lincoln sent General Grant into the battle.
6. Marcel gave a check and other gifts.
7. The three networks sent their best reporters to the scene.
8. A good student will read a newspaper every day.
9. The principal grabbed the dizzy student by the arm.
10. Many people enjoy a stroll through the woods.

EXERCISE 2

Create sentences to fit these diagrams. Then write each one on the correct diagram.

1.

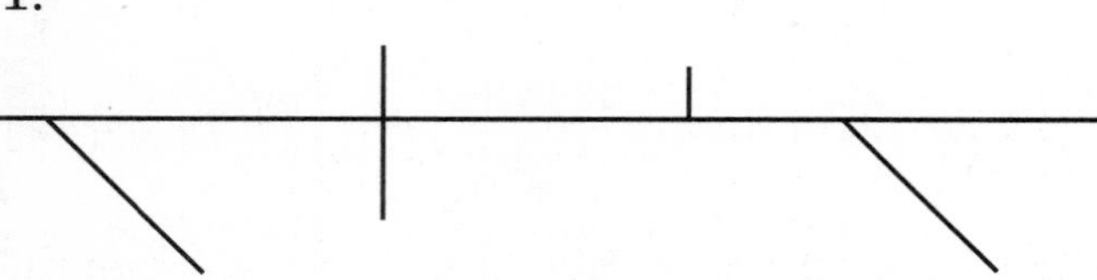

2.

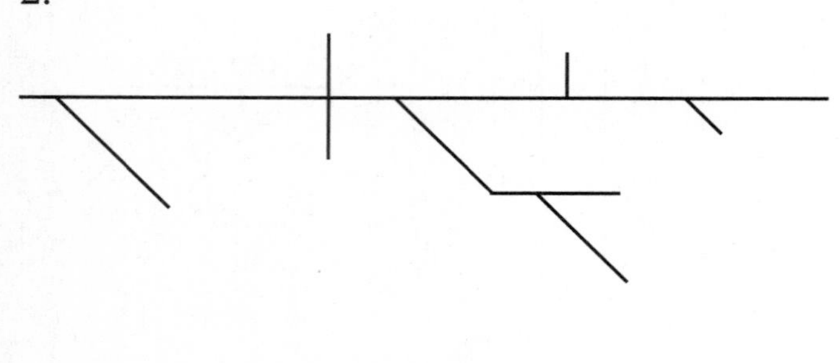

3.

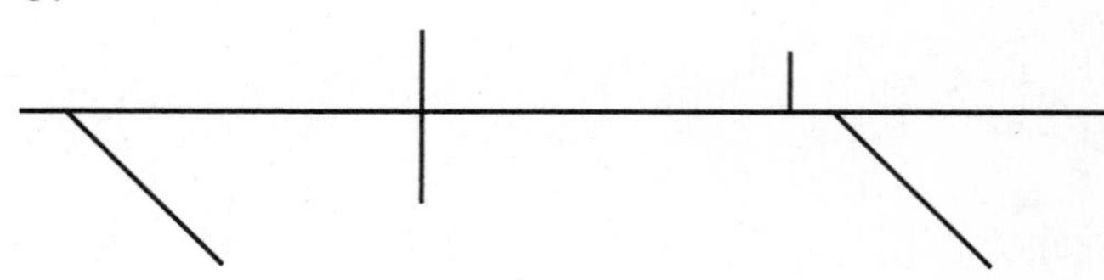

4.

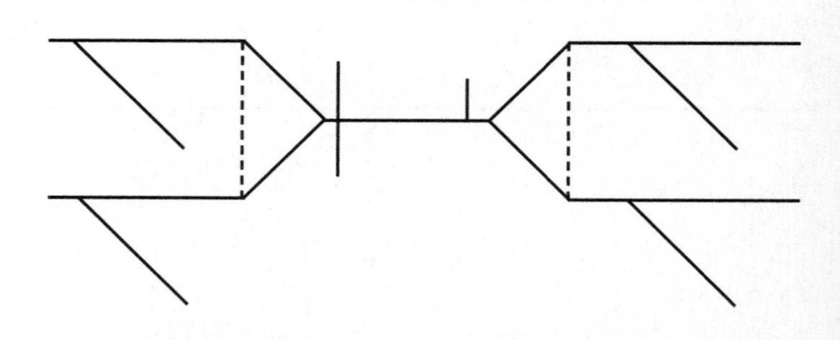

EXERCISE 3

Name________________________________

Unscramble the following groups of words to make complete sentences and then diagram.

1. sister asked cake for my the recipe her ________________________________
2. need Casey paper some will________________________________
3. most CD player I expensive bought the store the in________________________________
4. opened Pete Denver store piano in a________________________________
5. recommended Nora great a book ________________________________

EXERCISE 4

Find the mistakes in the following diagrams. Then, on a sheet of paper, diagram the sentences correctly.

1. The fire cast strange shadows across the room.

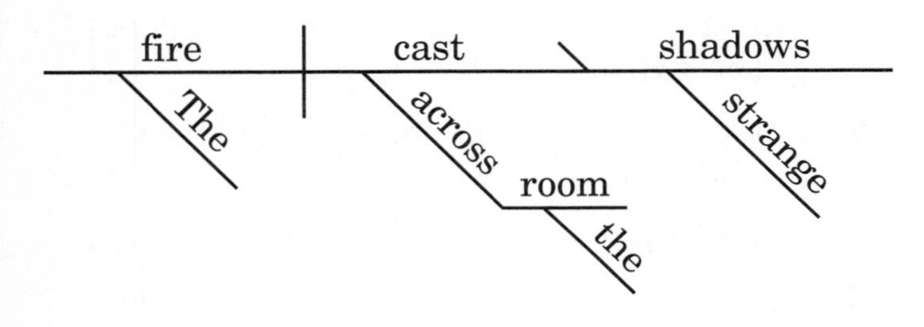

2. The choir bought new outfits for the concert.

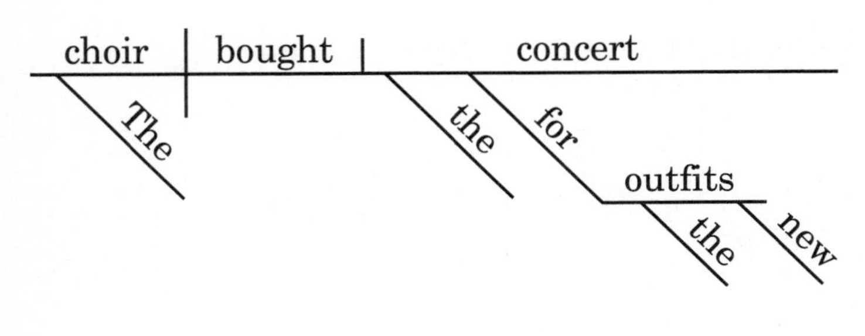

3. The sleigh rails hit the roof with a loud bang.

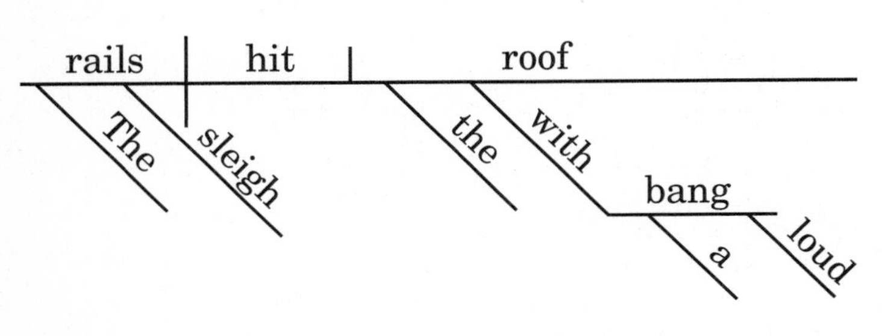

4. Ellen handled the hot torch with ease.

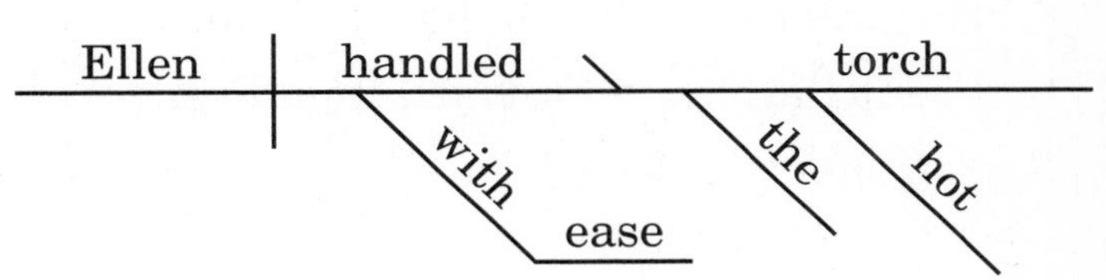

5. The disc jockey picked his favorite song on the list.

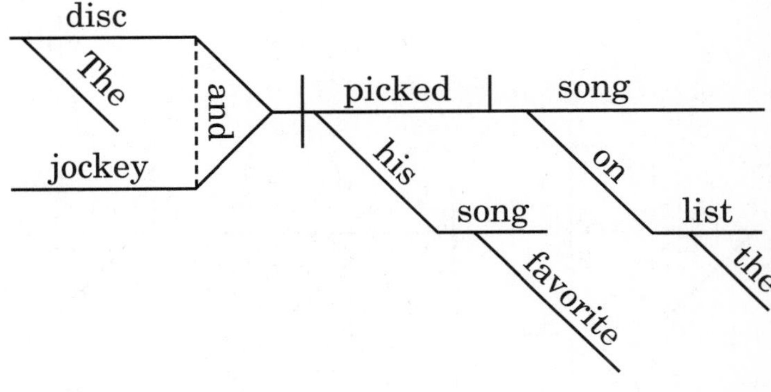

Indirect Objects

Name________________________

An indirect object is always placed below the verb on a line parallel to the verb and connected to it by a slanted line. Modifiers of the indirect object are placed on slanted lines directly beneath it.

Examples:

I gave them a piece of paper.

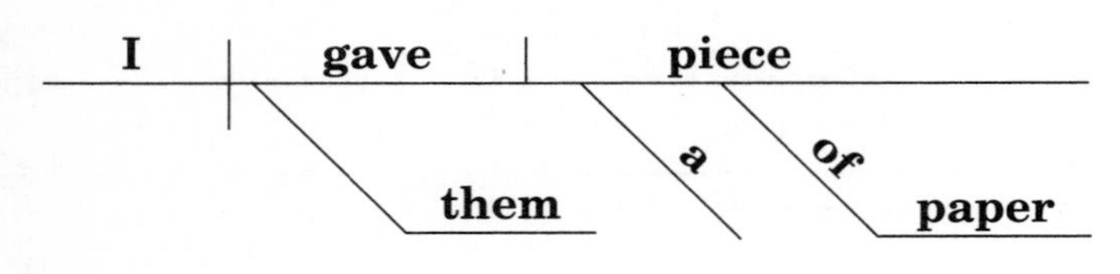

You should write your friend a letter.

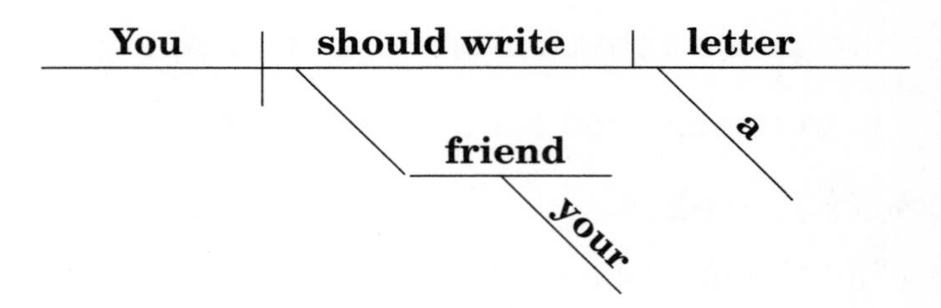

EXERCISE 1

In the following sentences, underline the verbs once, the direct objects twice, and the indirect objects three times. Then diagram the sentences.

1. She gives me a pain.
2. Paul told them the bad news.
3. The director taught the choir a new song.
4. He gave Sharon a symbol of his love.
5. I sent Barbara a postcard from France.
6. You should not feed the geese that corn.
7. The star goalie left his sister two tickets at the gate.
8. The boss handed his laziest employee the broom.
9. Anne Frank's diary won her instant fame.
10. The huge picture window in the room offered everyone a good view.

EXERCISE 2

Create sentences to fit these diagrams. Then write each one on the correct diagram.

1.

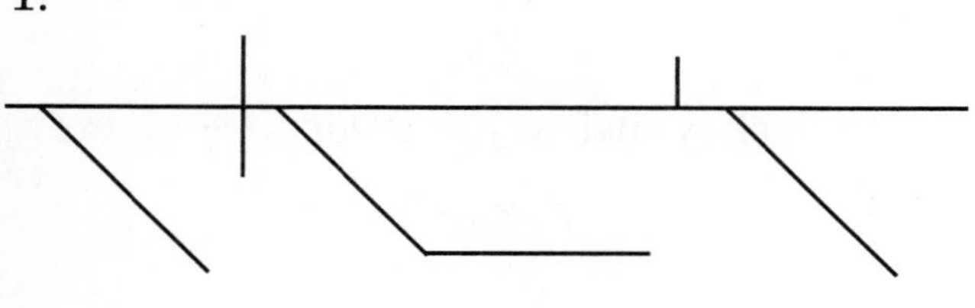

2.

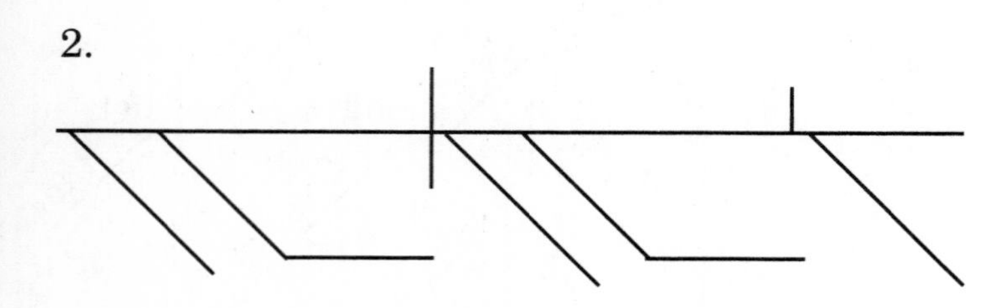

3.

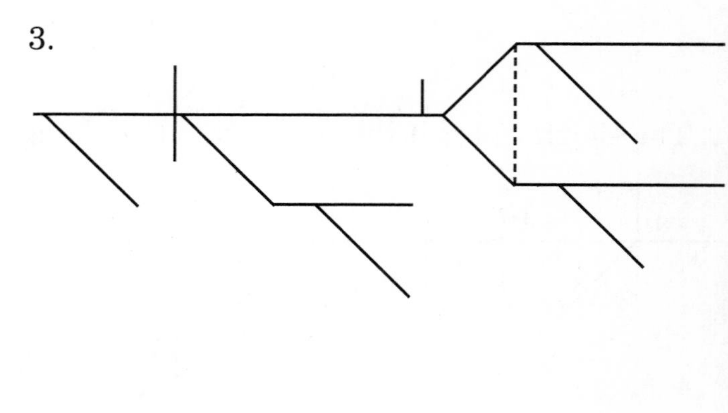

EXERCISE 3

Name____________________________

Unscramble the following groups of words to make complete sentences and then diagram.

1. him secret told she an interesting ____________________________
2. sent grandmother me shirt a my for Christmas ____________________________
3. served Luigi Chef Terry delicious a pizza dinner for ____________________________
4. you doctor anything about that tell not can surgery ____________________________
5. with builder their guaranteed homes the homeowners satisfaction the ____________________________

EXERCISE 4

Find the mistakes in the following diagrams. Then, on a sheet of paper, diagram the sentences correctly.

1. The referee's decision left us a choice.

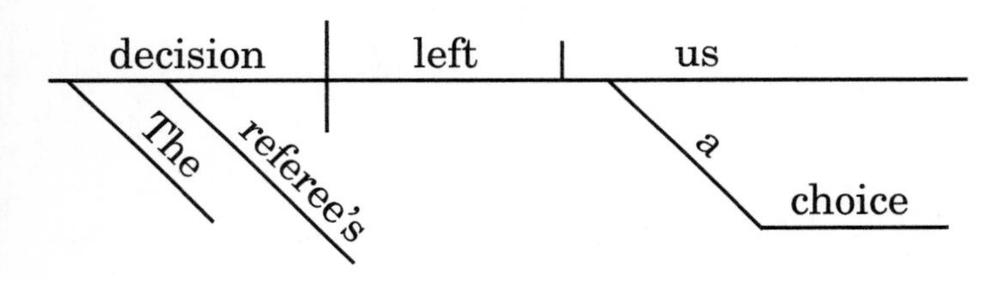

2. We will bake my aunt a birthday cake.

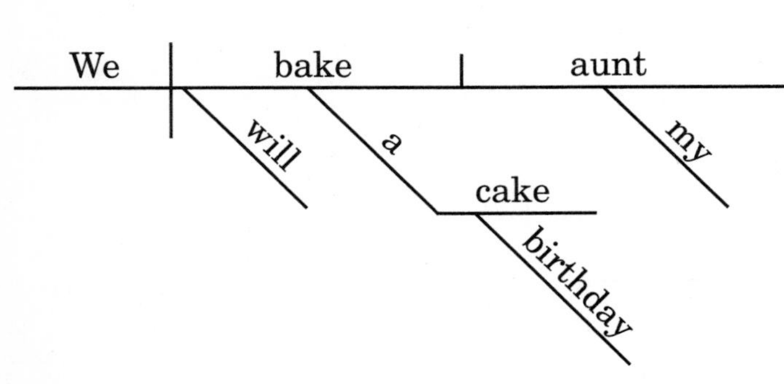

3. My sister handed my brother his football.

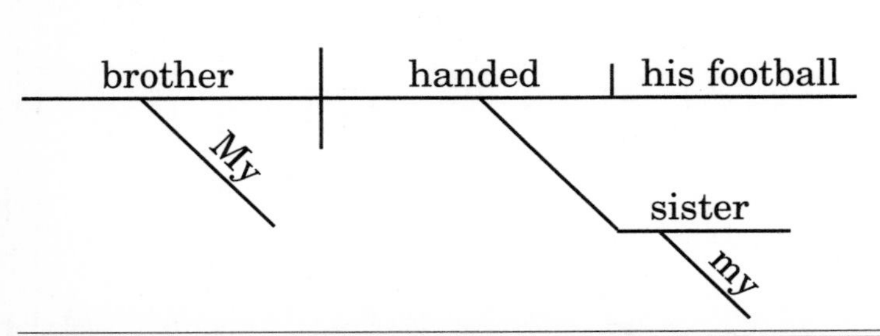

4. The waiter ordered the woman a plate of chop suey.

waiter | ordered | chop suey

The, woman, the, a, of, plate

5. I built my dad a wooden lawn chair for Father's Day.

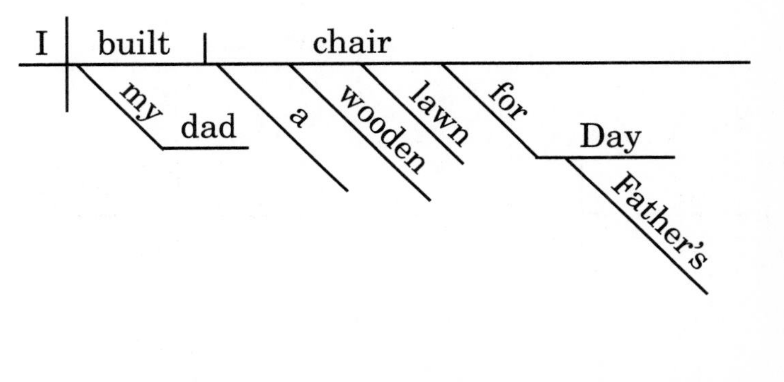

Objective Complements

Name______________________________________

An objective complement is placed on the same line as the subject, verb, and direct object. It is separated from the direct object by a line slanting back toward the direct object.

Examples:

The people elected him president.

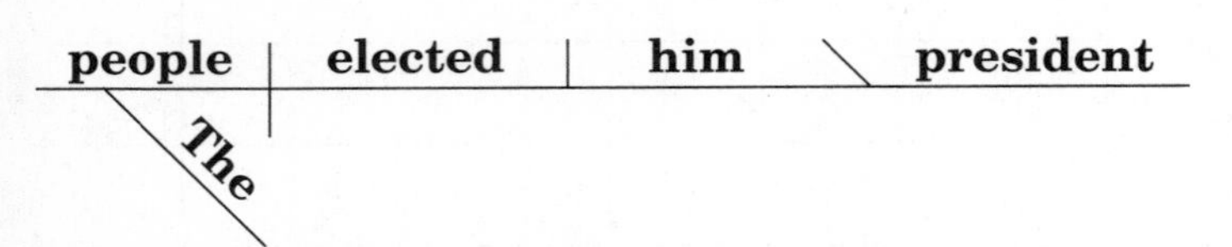

The referee declared the contest invalid.

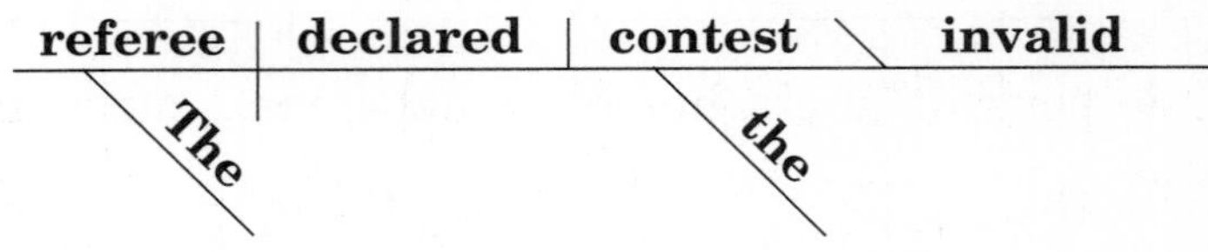

EXERCISE 1

In the following sentences, underline the verbs once, the direct objects twice, and the objective complements three times. Then diagram the sentences.

1. They made Greg spokesman for the company.
2. I am painting this room green.
3. Tom labeled all of the packages fragile.
4. Mom calls my brother stubborn.
5. We will make Heather goalie.
6. She named the new kitten Hodo.
7. The fans chose Ozzie best player on the team.
8. The hikers found the cave good protection from the storm.
9. The departure of Marilyn and Jud made the party a disaster.
10. Jim finds all books worthwhile.

EXERCISE 2

Create sentences to fit these diagrams. Then write each one on the correct diagram.

1.

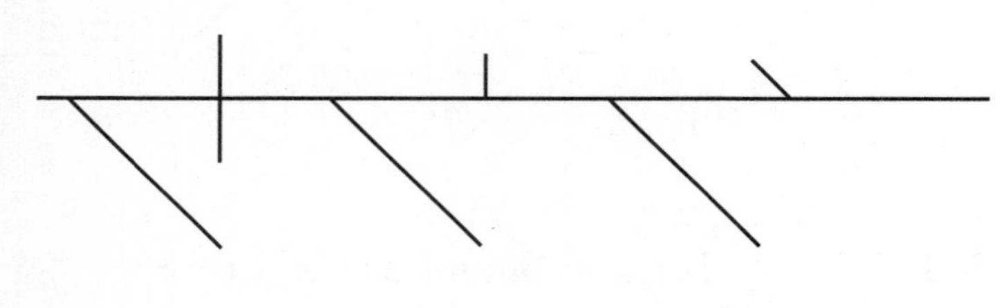

2.

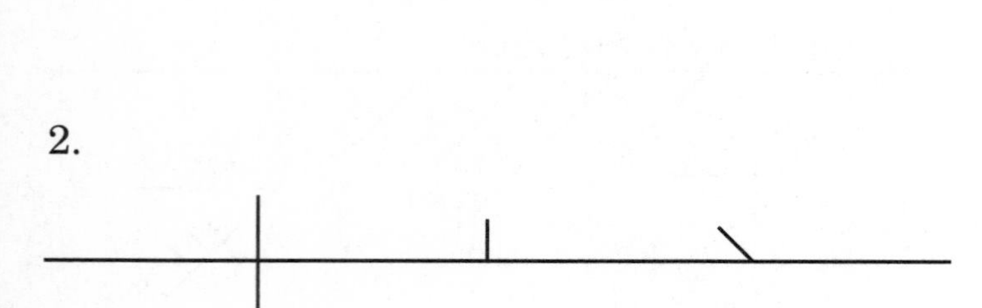

3.

EXERCISE 3

Name______________________________

Unscramble the following groups of words to make complete sentences and then diagram.

1. labeled John good very a worker they ______________________________
2. cast diverse the made play attractive the ______________________________
3. made he house modest a ranch the ______________________________
4. chose Alan team the captain ______________________________
5. called his Frank Lloyd Wright building landmark architectural an ______________________________

____

EXERCISE 4

Find the mistakes in the following diagrams. Then, on a sheet of paper, diagram the sentences correctly.

1. They considered Harvey the star of the show.

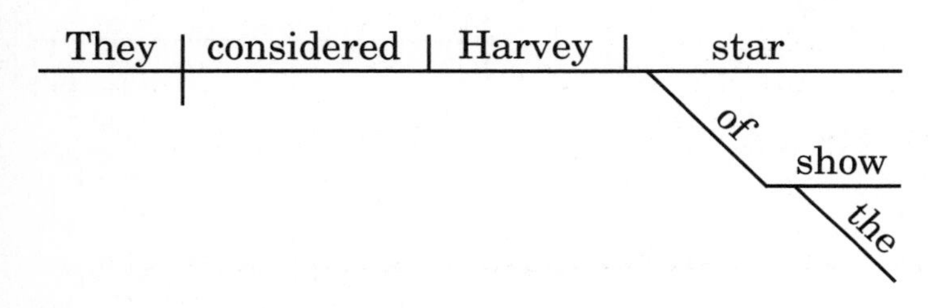

2. The mayor appointed Maria chief.

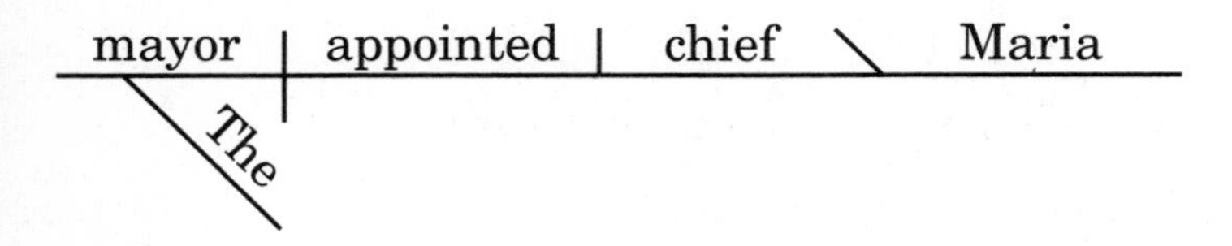

3. The town council will appoint Jed mayor this evening.

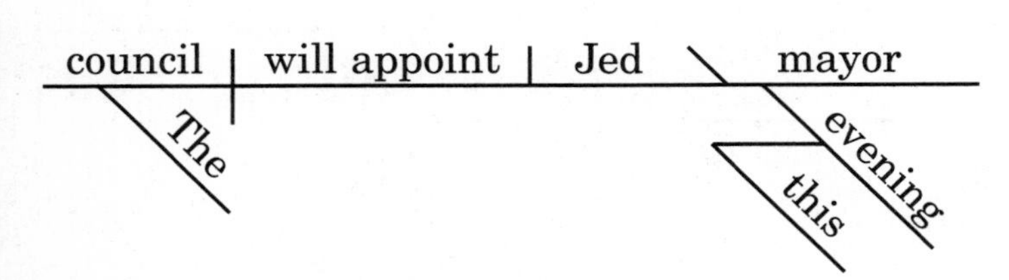

4. We will elect Billy alderman.

We | will elect \ Billy | alderman

5. The judge ruled the decision void.

judge | ruled | decision void
The
the

Compound Subjects

Name________________________

REVIEW EXERCISE 1

In the following sentences, underline the subjects once and the verbs twice. Then diagram the sentences.

1. My pencil and eraser disappeared.
2. A car and driver were entered.
3. An ape and an aardvark escaped.
4. Greg and Vytas celebrated.
5. The oranges and kiwis were squashed.

REVIEW EXERCISE 2

Create sentences to fit these diagrams. Then write each one on the correct diagram.

1.

2.

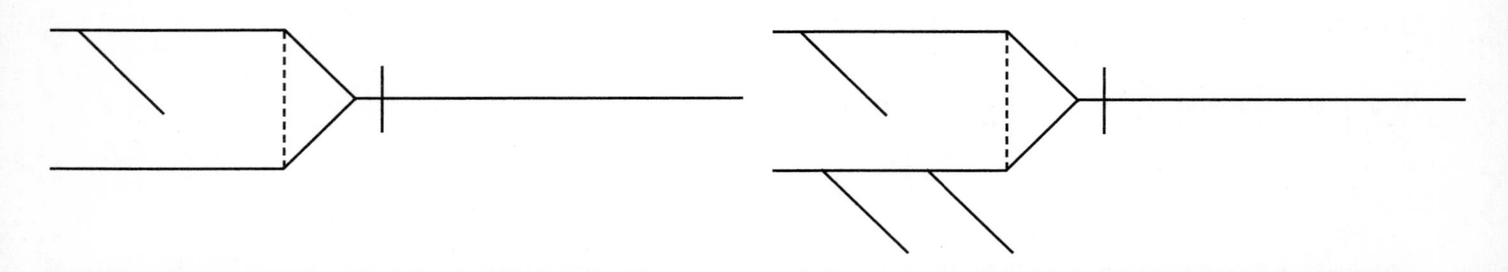

Compound Verbs

REVIEW EXERCISE 1

In the following sentences, underline the subjects once and the verbs twice. Then diagram the sentences.

1. The girl and the boy shifted and fidgeted.
2. The house and the car were bought and sold.
3. Burgers and fries were purchased and distributed.
4. Henri listens and observes.
5. John can read and comprehend.

REVIEW EXERCISE 2

Create sentences to fit these diagrams. Then write each one on the correct diagram.

1.

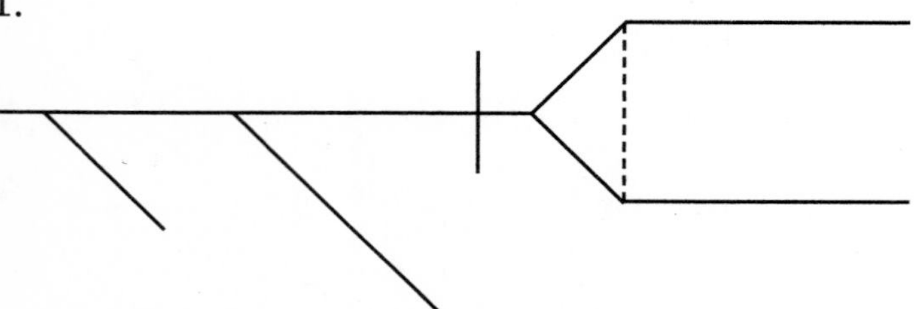

2.

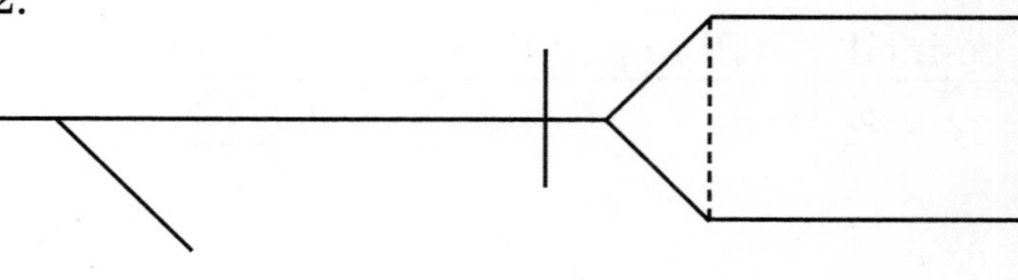

Adjective Modifiers

Name____________________

REVIEW EXERCISE 1

In the following sentences, underline the adjectives and then diagram the sentences.

1. The big, yellow bus arrived.
2. Green beans will grow.
3. The vicious dog attacked.
4. A warm hat will help.
5. A kind, old man and a young boy conversed.

REVIEW EXERCISE 2

Create sentences to fit these diagrams. Then write each one on the correct diagram.

1. 2.

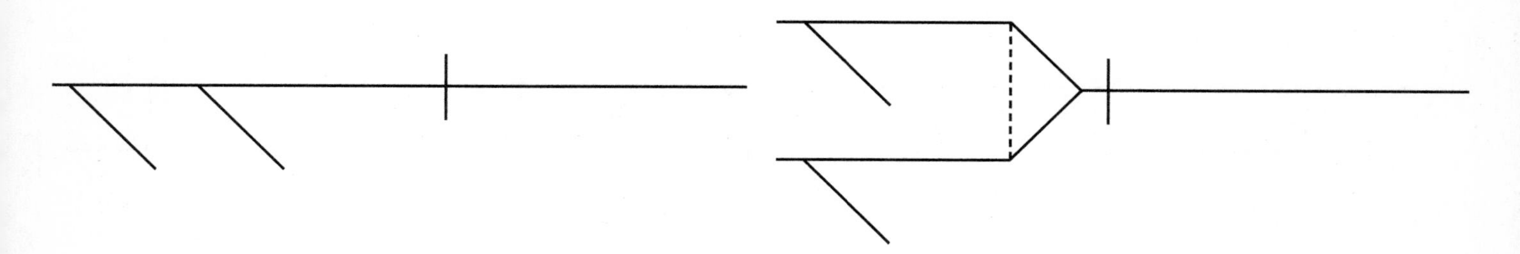

Adverb Modifiers

REVIEW EXERCISE 1

In the following sentences, underline the adverbs and then diagram the sentences.

1. He ran quickly and jumped high.
2. Doris studied very hard.
3. Her small, round mouth opened wide.
4. The red gate slammed shut.
5. Jonathan paced nervously.

REVIEW EXERCISE 2

Create sentences to fit these diagrams. Then write each one on the correct diagram.

1.

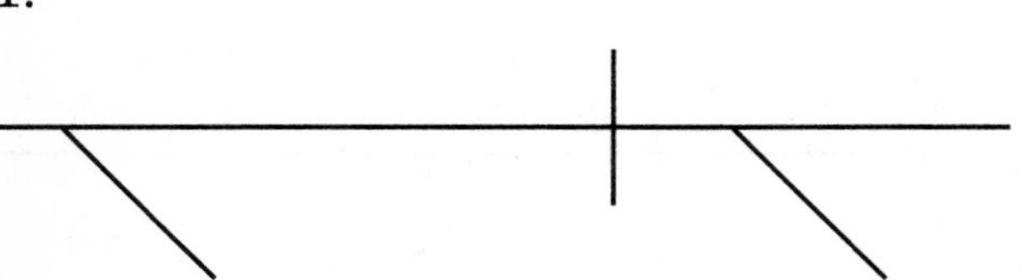

2.

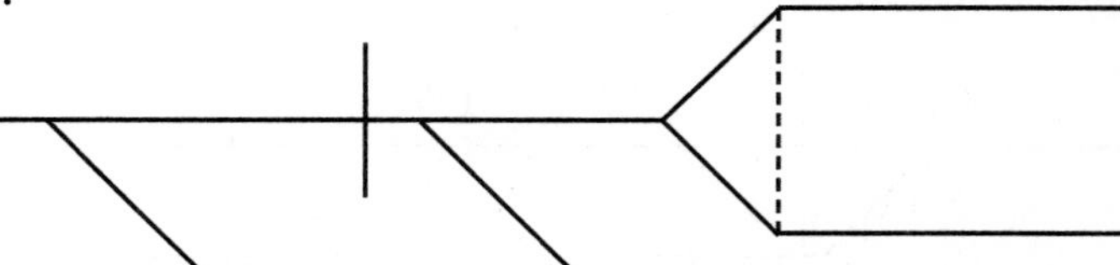

Adjective Prepositional Phrases

Name________________________

REVIEW EXERCISE 1

In the following sentences, underline the prepositions once and their objects twice. Then diagram the sentences.

1. The car with the red racing stripe won.
2. The plane on the deck of the carrier disappeared yesterday.
3. The girl beside my brother fell down.
4. The processor inside the computer failed.
5. The old car without air conditioning sizzled.

REVIEW EXERCISE 2

Create sentences to fit these diagrams. Then write each one on the correct diagram.

1.

2.

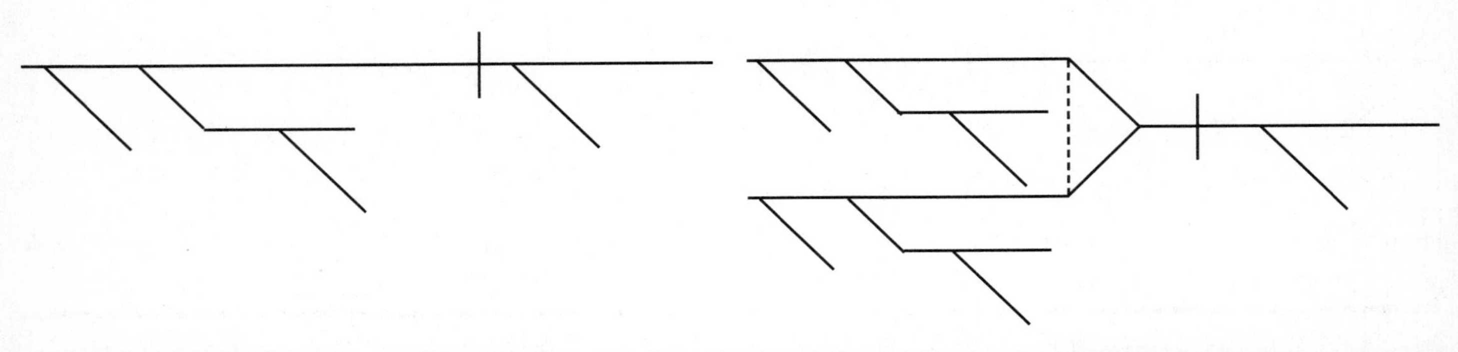

Adverb Prepositional Phrases

REVIEW EXERCISE 1

In the following sentences, underline the prepositions once and their objects twice. Then diagram the sentences.

1. Our biology class went to the zoo.
2. The jet flew above the clouds.
3. The nuclear submarine dove under the reef.
4. The fighter in the red trunks was hit squarely on the chin.
5. The boy in the soapbox car raced down the hill.

REVIEW EXERCISE 2

Create sentences to fit these diagrams. Then write each one on the correct diagram.

1.

2.

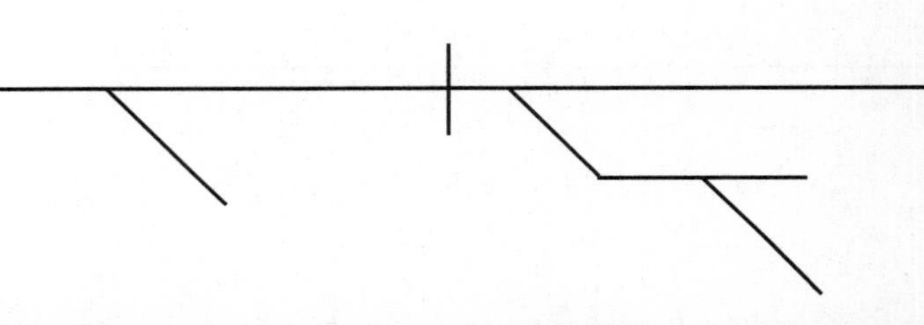

Subject Complements— Predicate Adjectives

Name________________________

REVIEW EXERCISE 1

In the following sentences, underline the predicate adjectives and then diagram the sentences.

1. The program was humorous.
2. The stadium was empty after the game.
3. Ted appeared delighted with the results of his final exam.
4. The meatballs smelled delicious to the hungry diners.
5. Mark should have been very happy after the meeting.

REVIEW EXERCISE 2

Create sentences to fit these diagrams. Then write each one on the correct diagram.

1.

2.

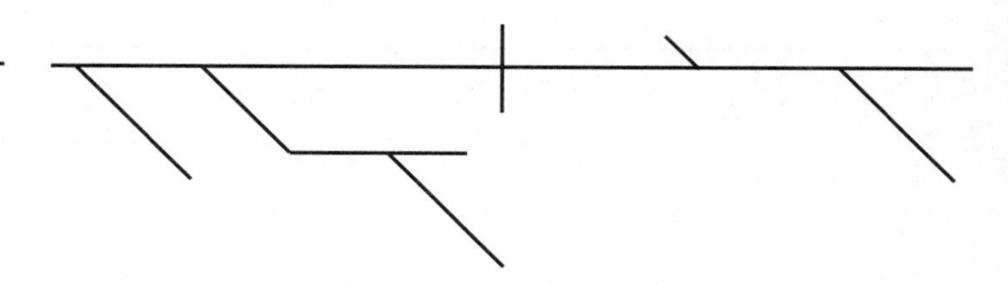

Subject Complements— Predicate Nouns

REVIEW EXERCISE 1

In the following sentences, underline the predicate nouns and then diagram the sentences.

1. Henry was the oldest player on the team.
2. His dog became a hero after the dramatic rescue.
3. Don is an excellent worker.
4. Bolivia is a very picturesque country.
5. Television has become a most effective medium.

REVIEW EXERCISE 2

Create sentences to fit these diagrams. Then write each one on the correct diagram.

1.

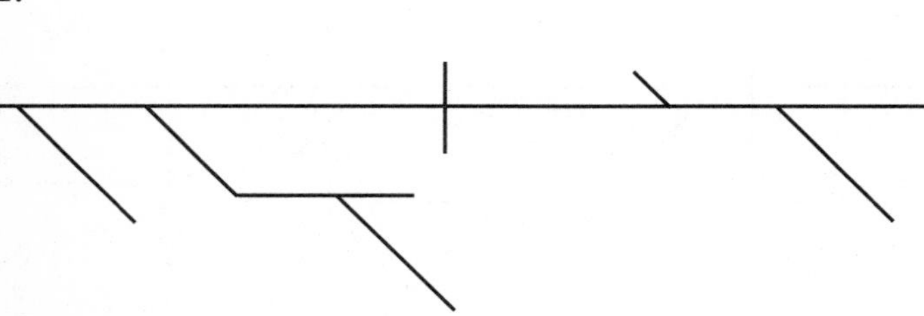

2.

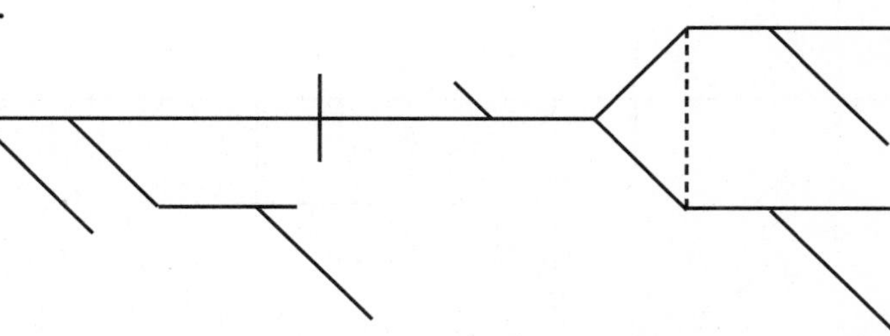

Direct Objects

Name____________________________

REVIEW EXERCISE 1

In the following sentences, underline the verbs once and the direct objects twice. Then diagram the sentences.

1. The outfielder hit the wall with a thud.
2. The goalie dove and stopped the ball.
3. The horse jumped the obstacle with ease.
4. Kenny accidentally slugged his friend squarely in the eye.
5. He served the ball over the net.

REVIEW EXERCISE 2

Create sentences to fit these diagrams. Then write each one on the correct diagram.

1.

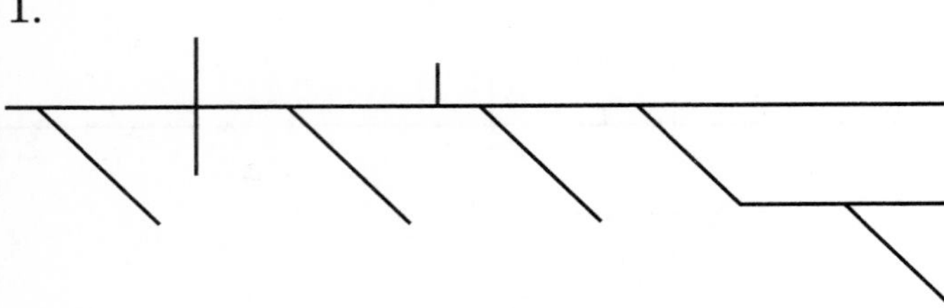

2.

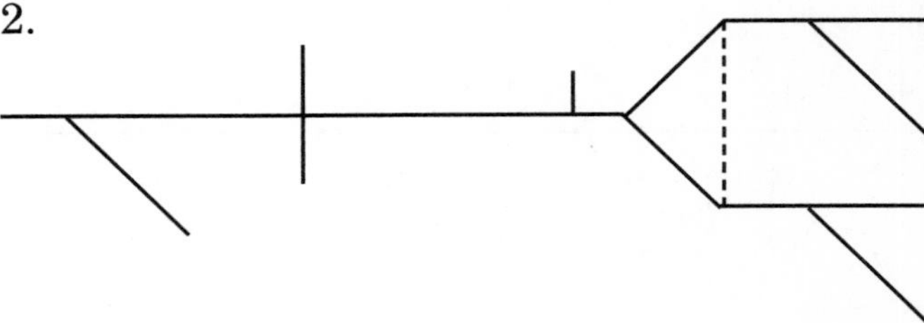

Indirect Objects

REVIEW EXERCISE 1

In the following sentences, underline the verbs once, the direct objects twice, and the indirect objects three times. Then diagram the sentences.

1. Melanie wrote her father a letter.
2. The waiter brought them four sandwiches.
3. Emily gave her mother a surprise party.
4. My aunt sent me two tickets to the ballet.
5. John's boss ordered him a brand-new car.

REVIEW EXERCISE 2

Create sentences to fit these diagrams. Then write each one on the correct diagram.

1.

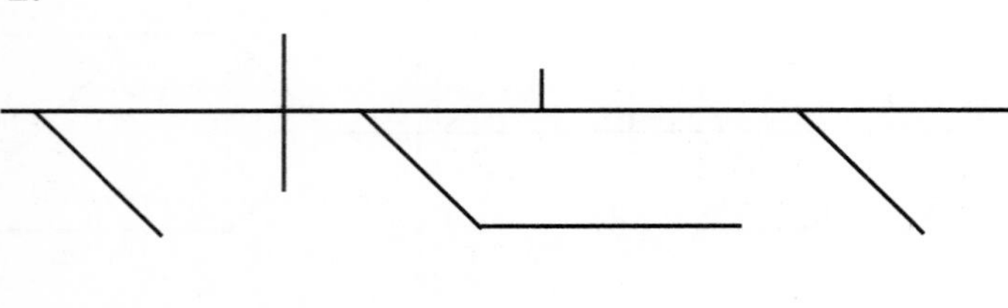

2.

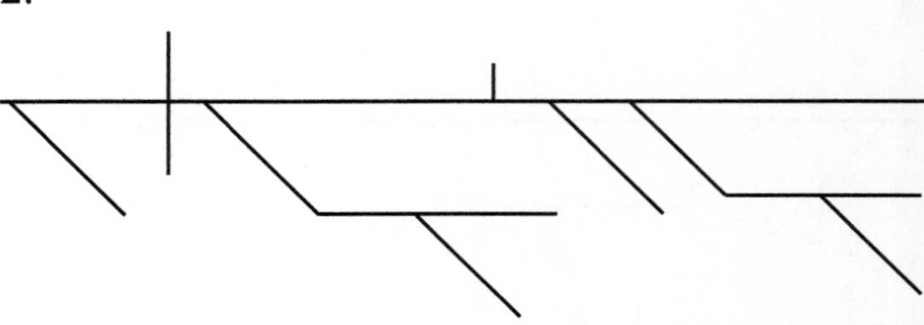

Appositives

Name______________________________

REVIEW EXERCISE 1

In the following sentences, underline the appositives once and their modifiers twice. Then diagram the sentences.

1. That man, the world's best father, is in the front.
2. Ohio, the Buckeye state, will be admitted.
3. Laurel and Hardy, silent film stars, attended.
4. Miriam, my best friend, flew to Milwaukee last night.
5. Joshua, a champion show dog, won in all categories.

REVIEW EXERCISE 2

Create sentences to fit these diagrams. Then write each one on the correct diagram.

1.

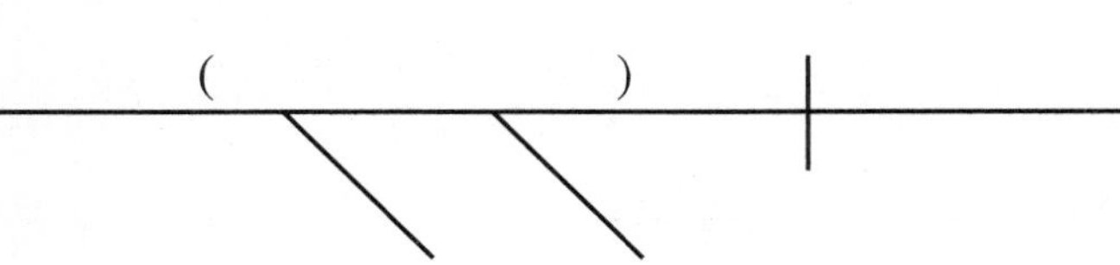

2.

Objective Complements

REVIEW EXERCISE 1

In the following sentences, underline the verbs once, the direct objects twice, and the objective complements three times. Then diagram the sentences.

1. I will never call you "Slim."
2. The extra chocolate made the cookies delicious.
3. We would not elect Darren dogcatcher.
4. One spectator called the game dull.
5. He would call that painting beautiful.

REVIEW EXERCISE 2

Create sentences to fit these diagrams. Then write each one on the correct diagram.

1.

2.

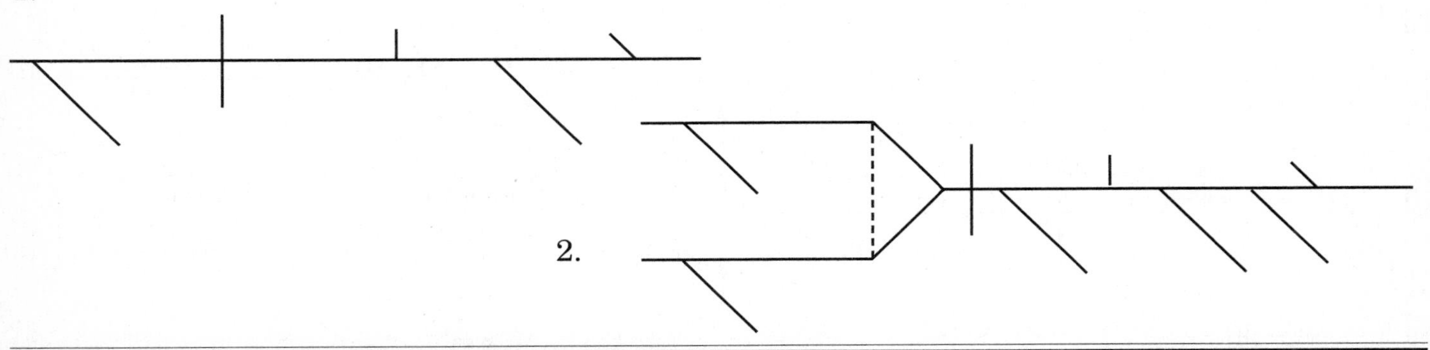

Answer Key

EXERCISE 1 — page 2

1. 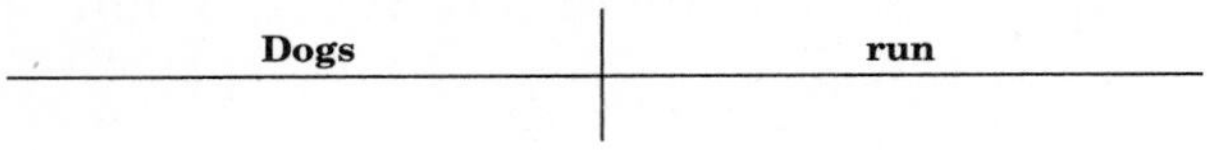 Dogs | run

2. 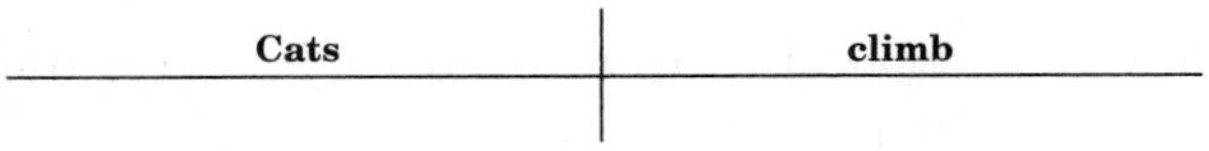 Cats | climb

3. 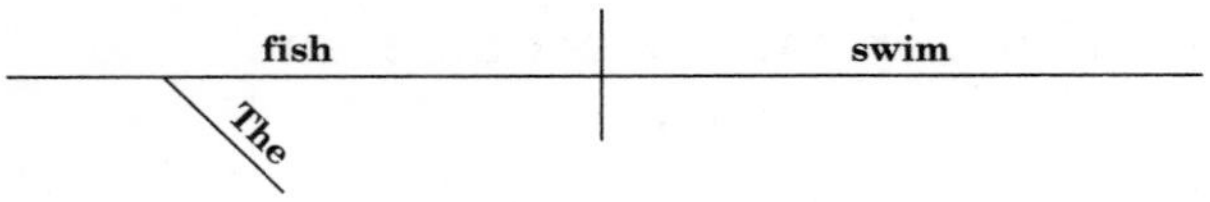 fish | swim
   The

4. 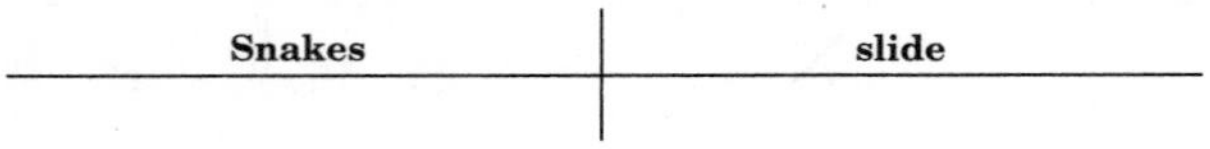 Snakes | slide

5. 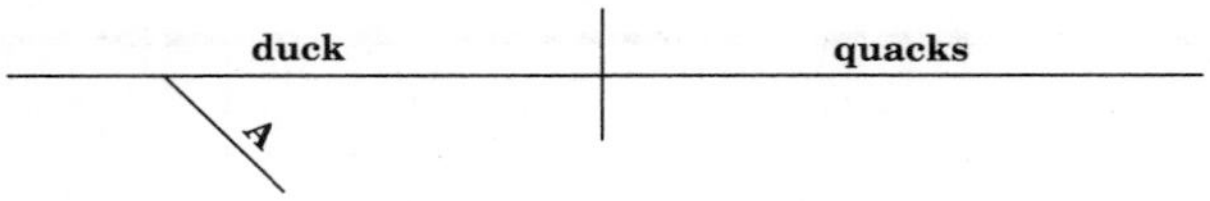 duck | quacks
   A

6. 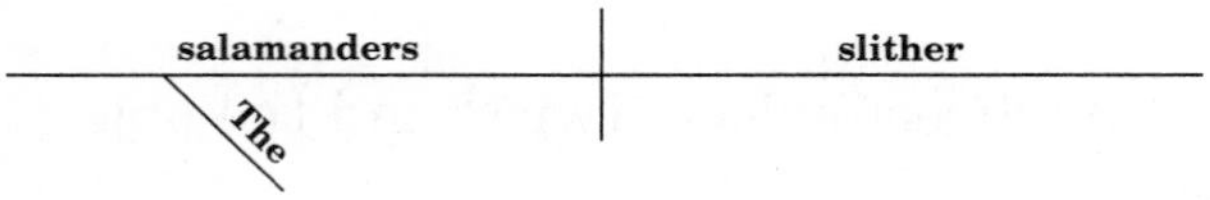 salamanders | slither
   The

7. 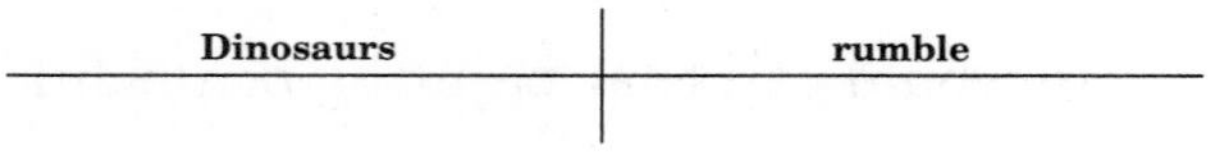 Dinosaurs | rumble

8.  Badgers | burrow

9. 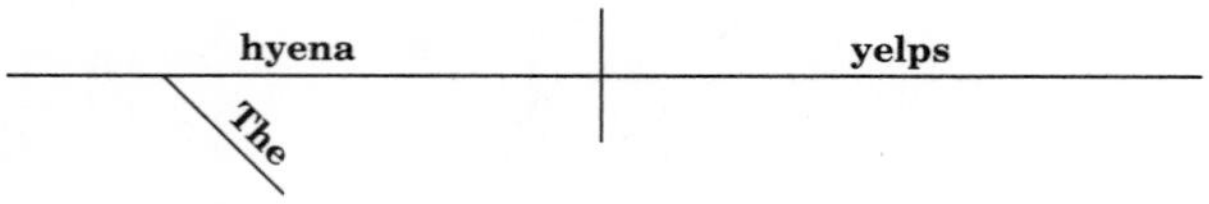 hyena | yelps
   The

10. 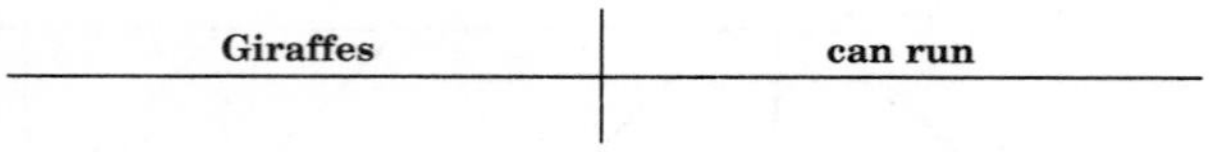 Giraffes | can run

EXERCISE 2 — page 2 (Answers will vary)

EXERCISE 3 — page 3

1. 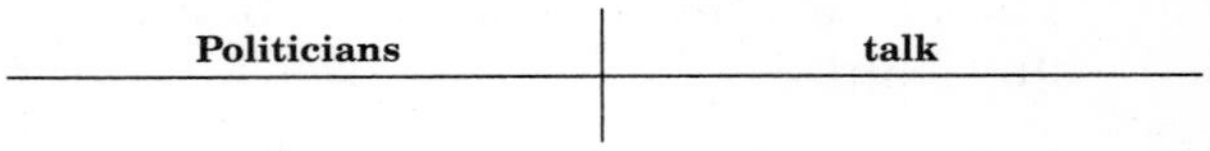 Politicians | talk

2.  Companies | advertise

3.  waiters | serve
   The

4.  Garbage | stinks

5. 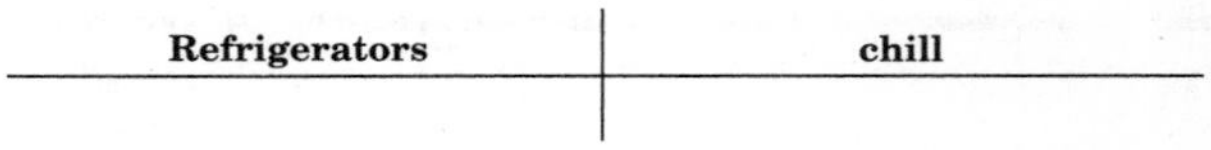 Refrigerators | chill

EXERCISE 4 — page 3

1. 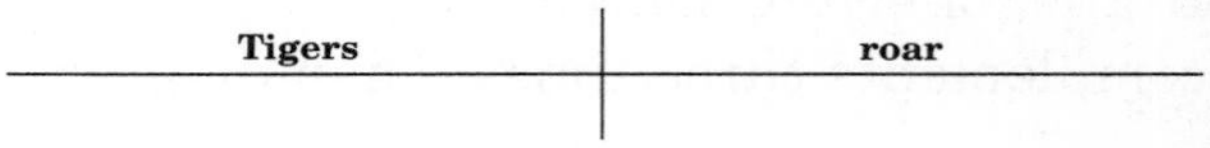 Tigers | roar

2.  Swallows | will return

3. 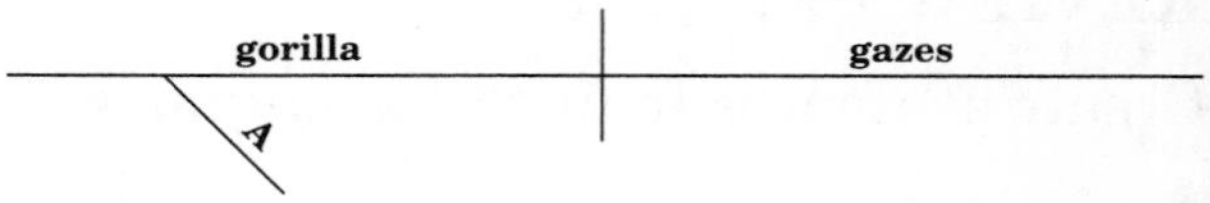 gorilla | gazes
   A

4. 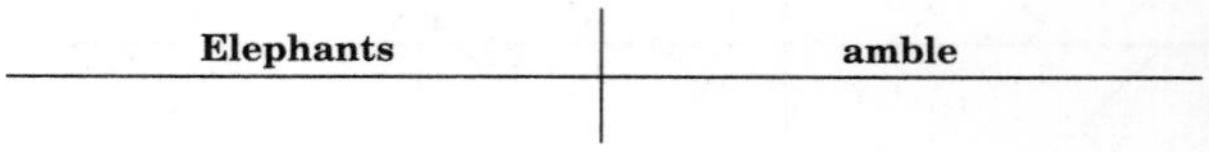 Elephants | amble

5. 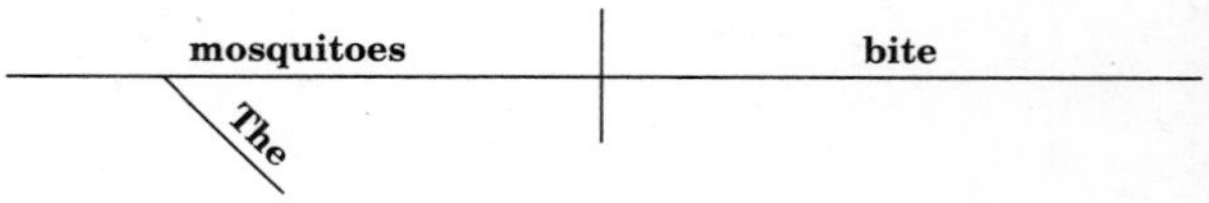 mosquitoes | bite
   The

Answer Key

EXERCISE 1 — page 4

1.

soldiers
The
and
fled
civilians
the

2.

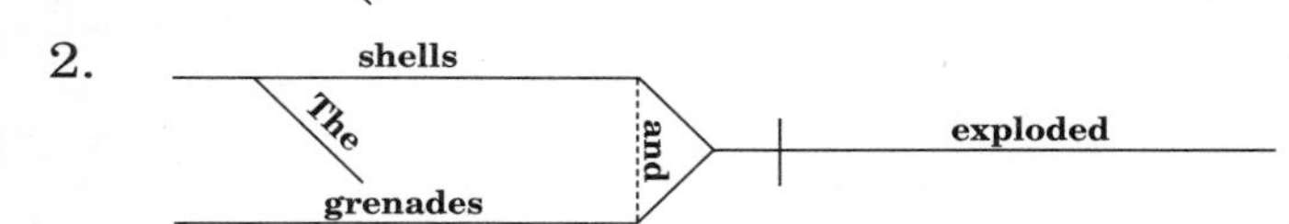

3.

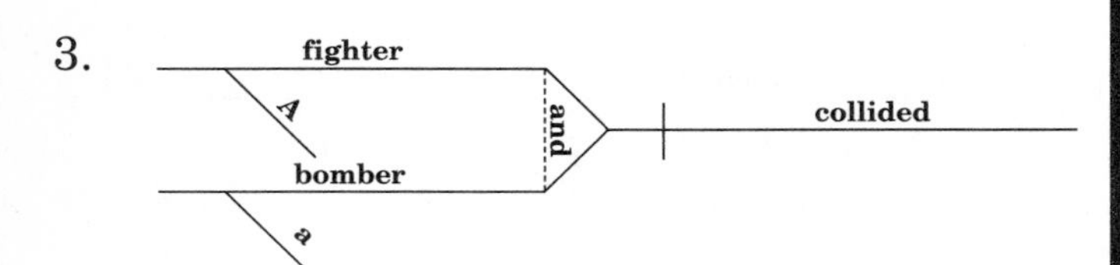

4.

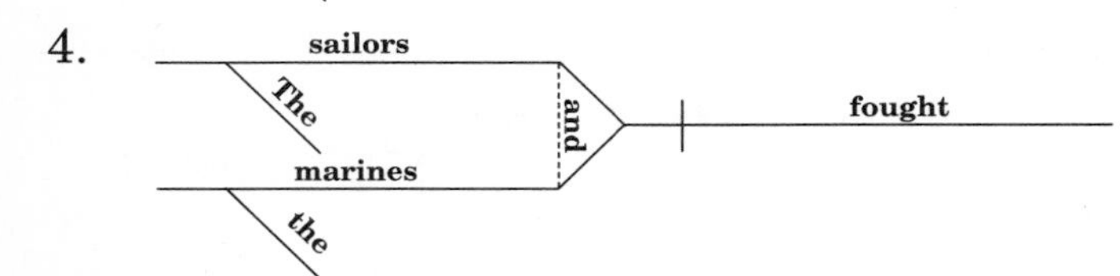

5.

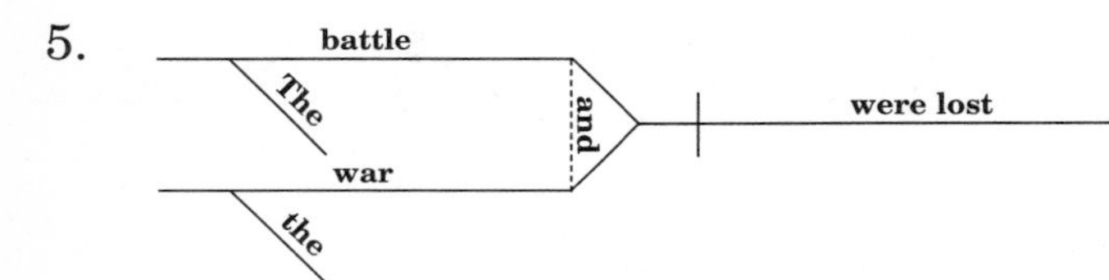

6.

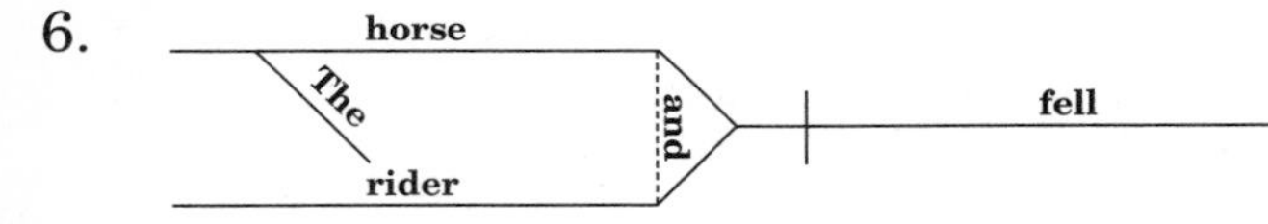

7.

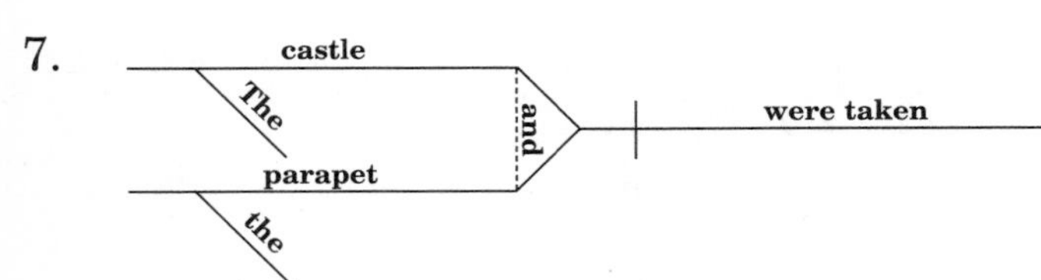

8.

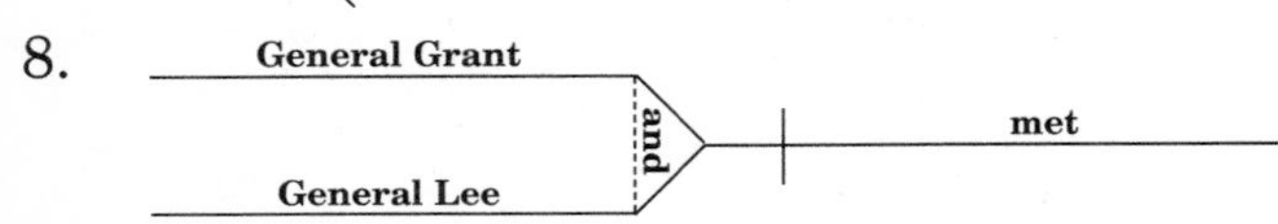

9.

10.

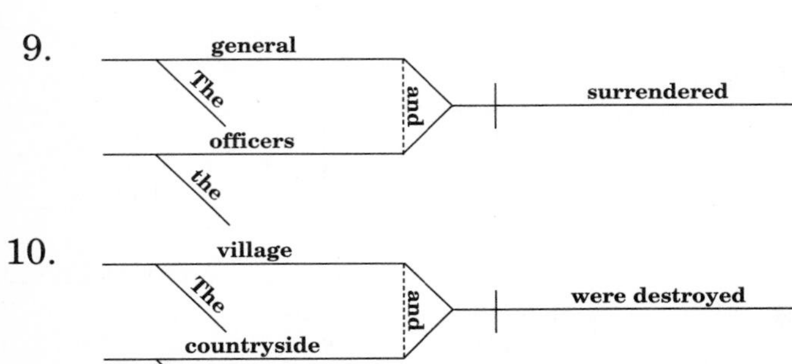

EXERCISE 2 — page 4 (Answers will vary)

EXERCISE 3 — page 5

1.

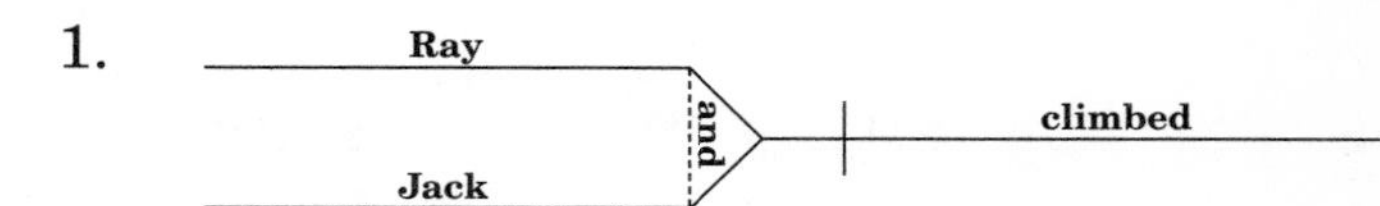

2.

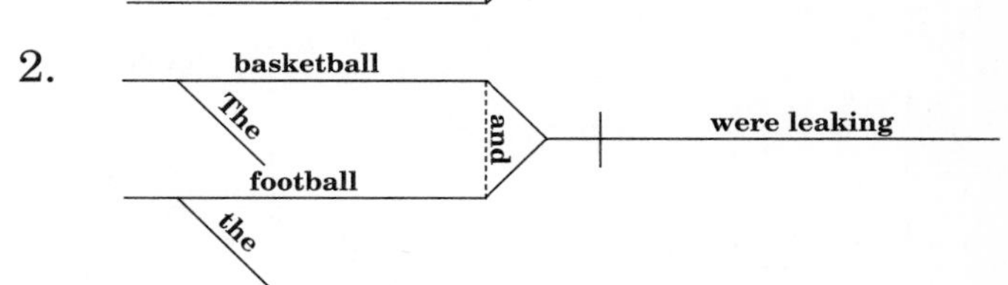

3.

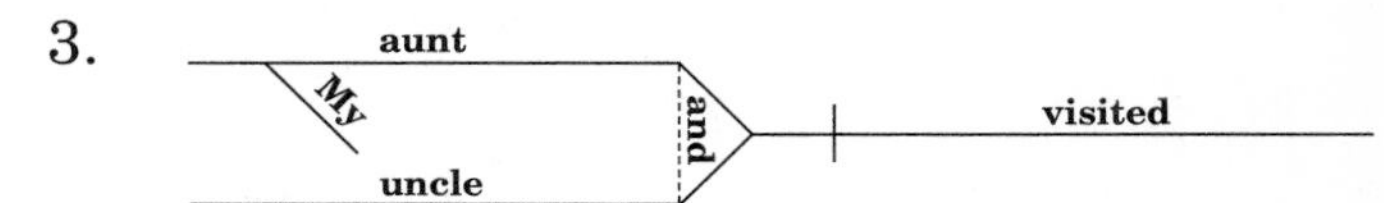

4.

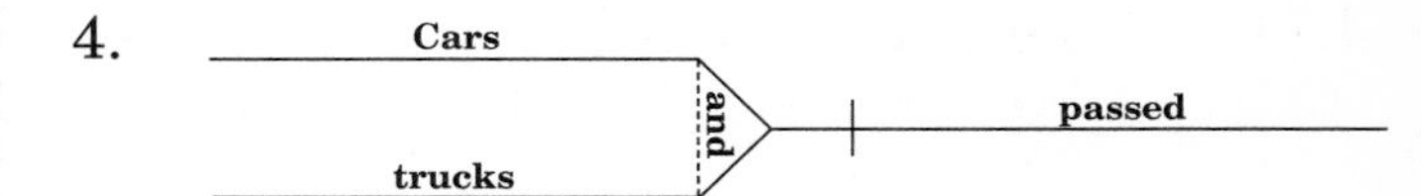

5.

Meteors
and
fell
asteroids

EXERCISE 4 — page 5

1.

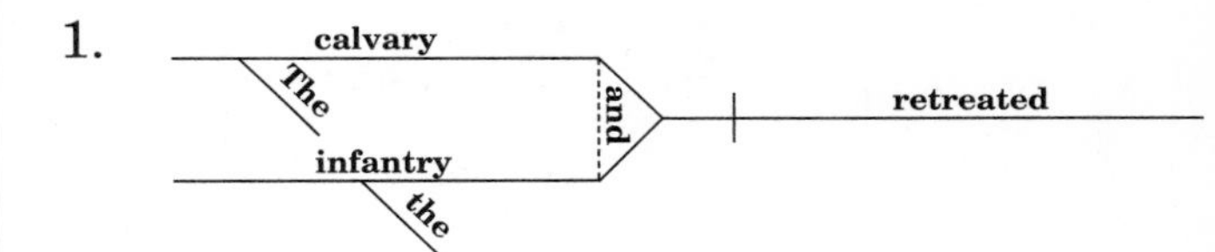

2.

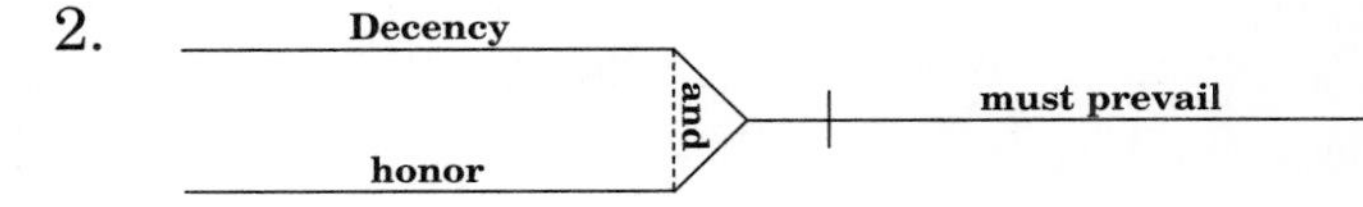

3.

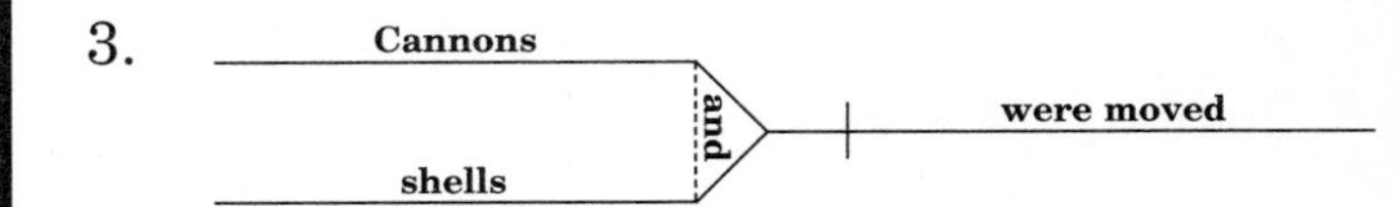

4.

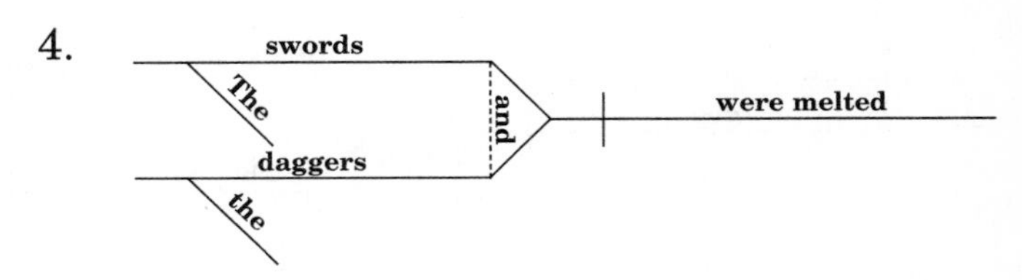

5.

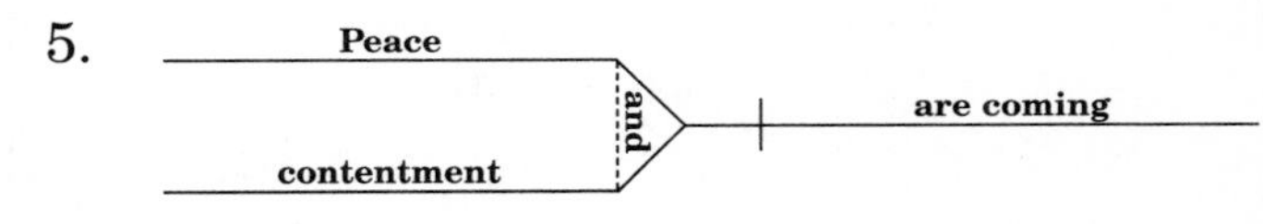

Answer Key

EXERCISE 1 — page 6

1.
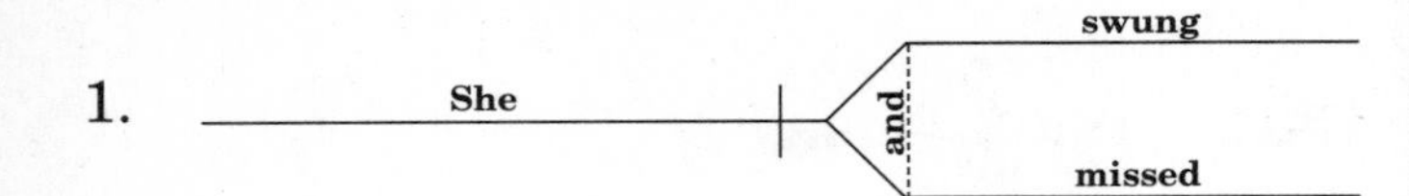

2.
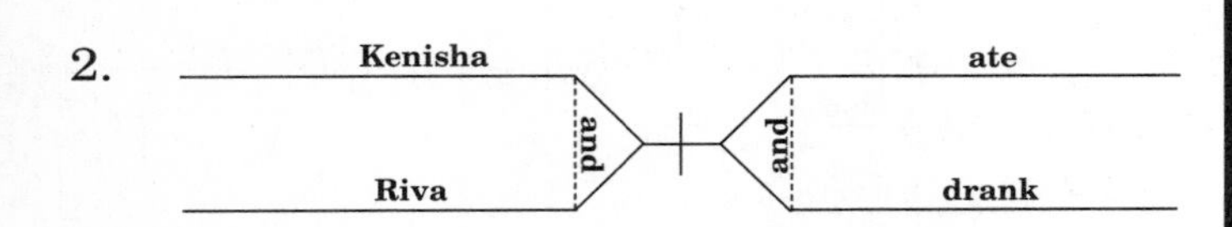

3.
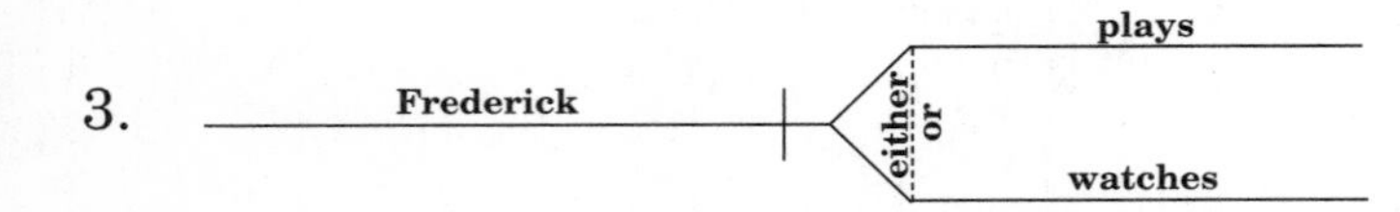

4.
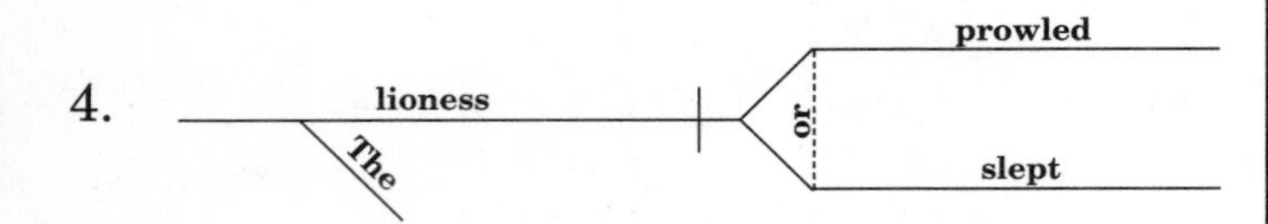

5.
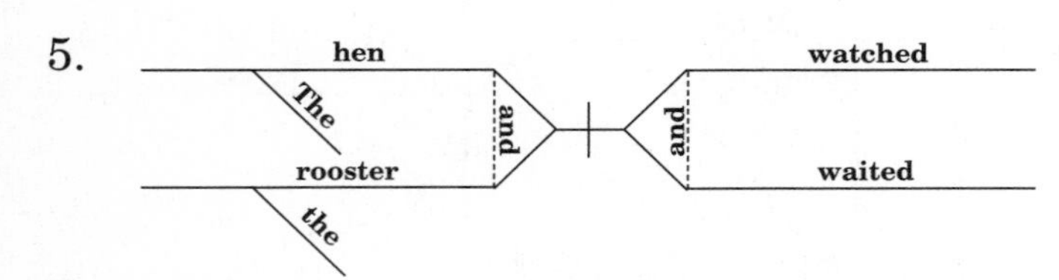

6.
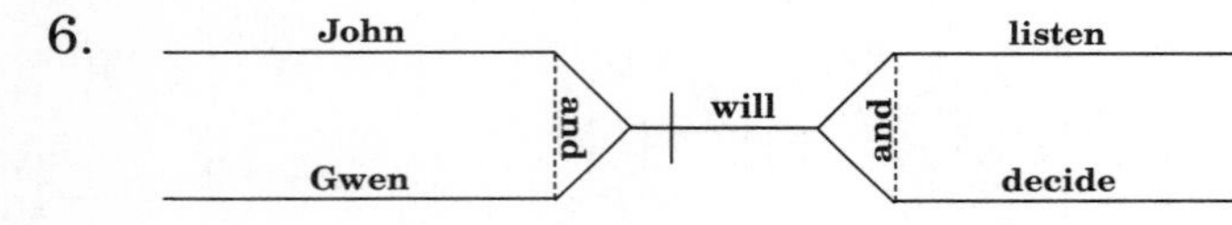

7.
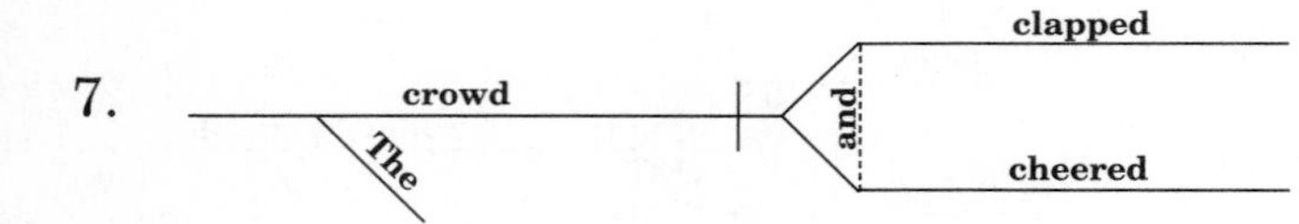

8.
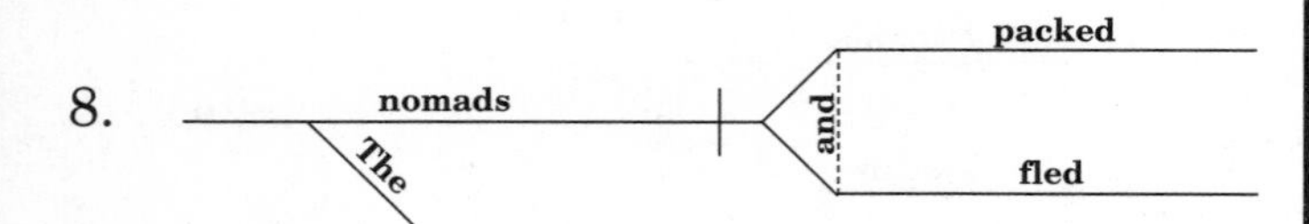

9.
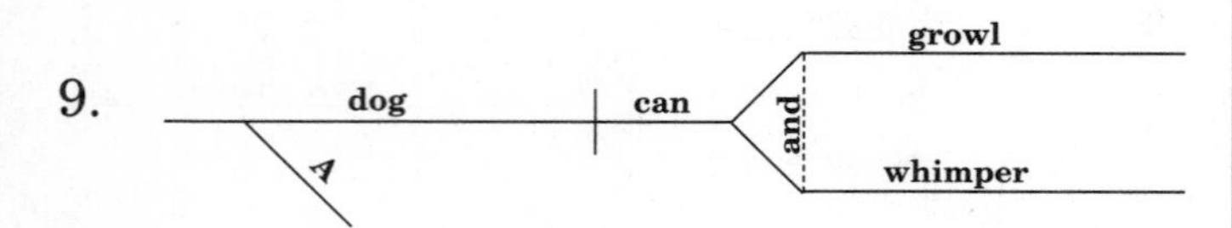

10.
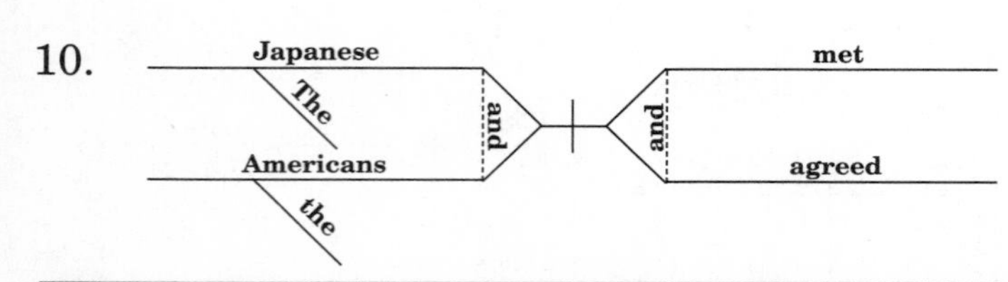

EXERCISE 2 — page 6 (Answers will vary)

EXERCISE 3 — page 7

1.
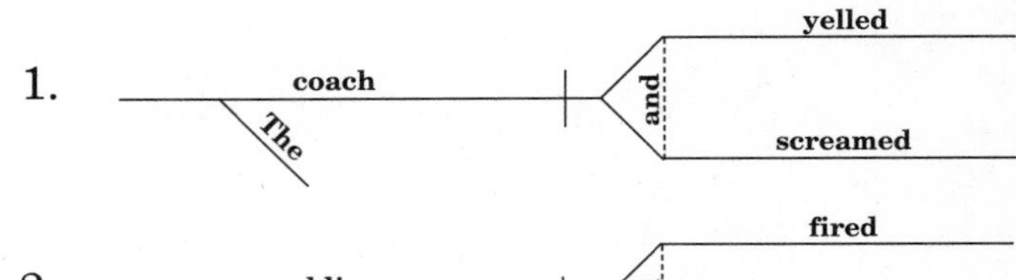

2.
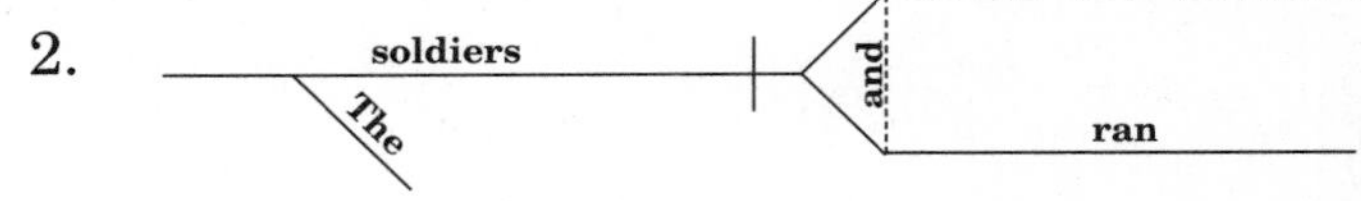

3.

4.
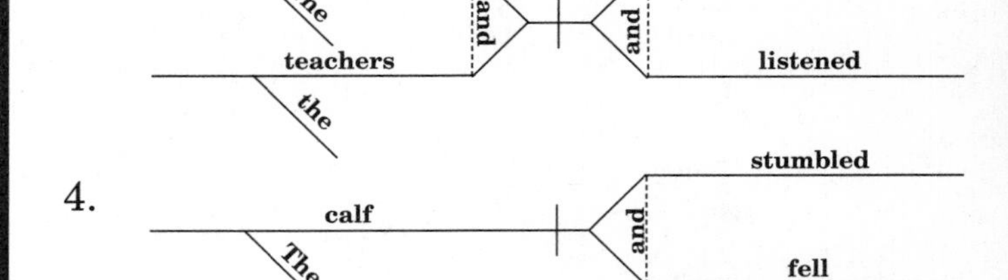

5.
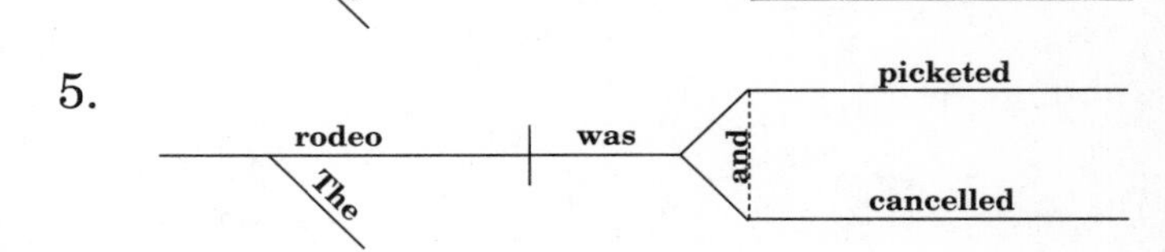

EXERCISE 4 — page 7

1.
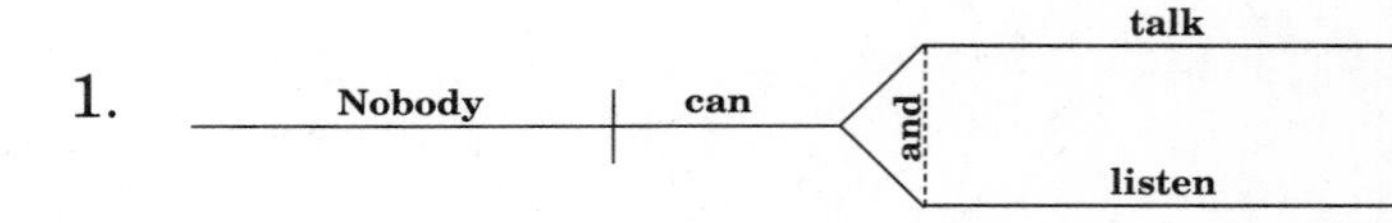

2.
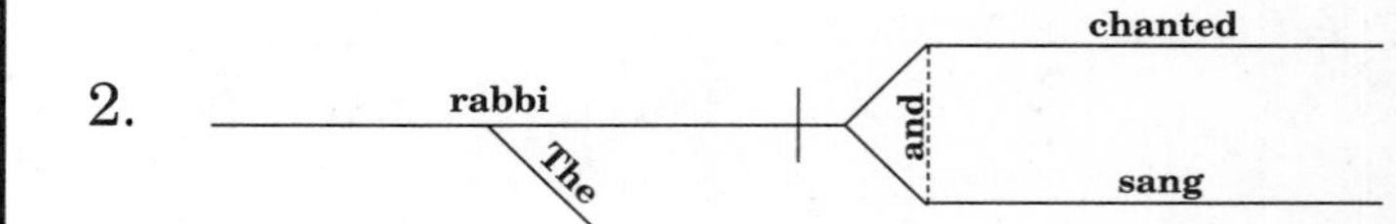

3.
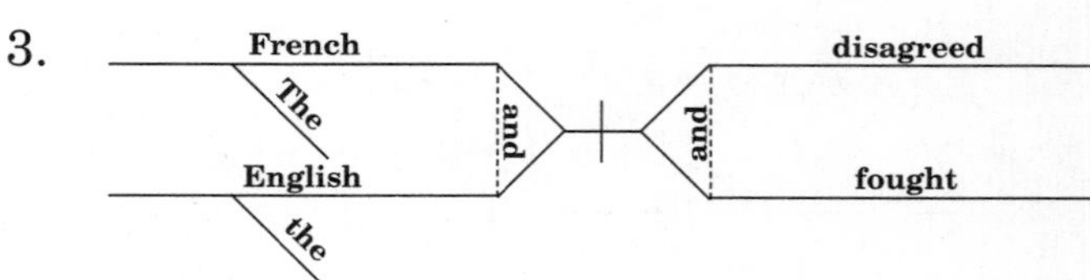

4.
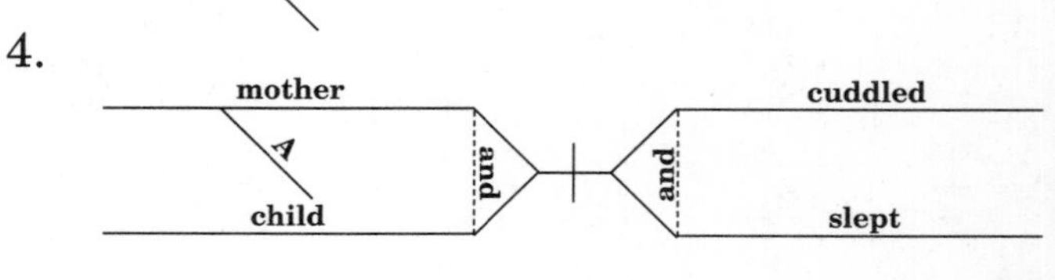

5.
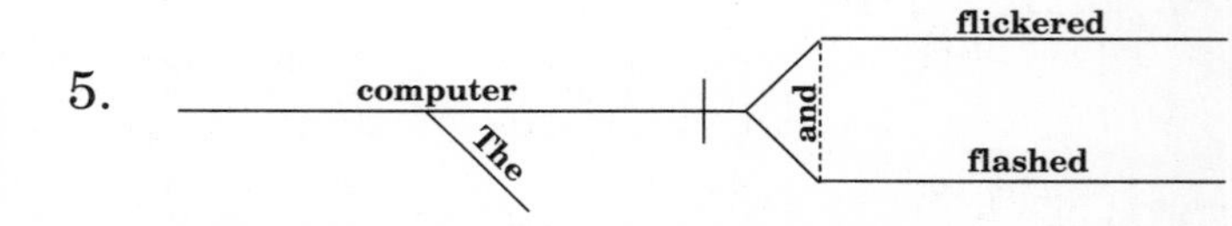

Answer Key

EXERCISE 1 — page 8

1.

ship | will roll
A
big

2.

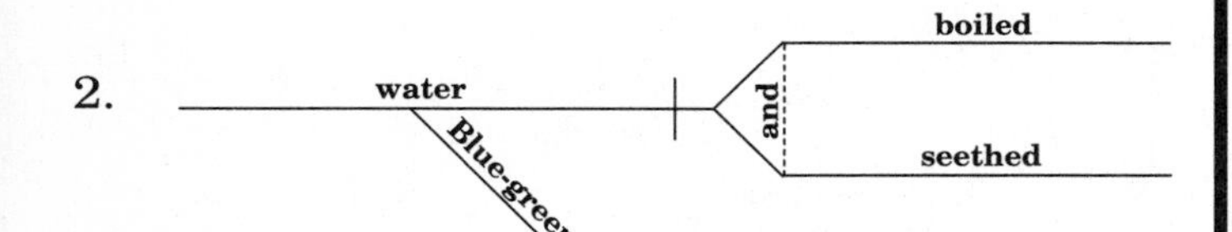

3.

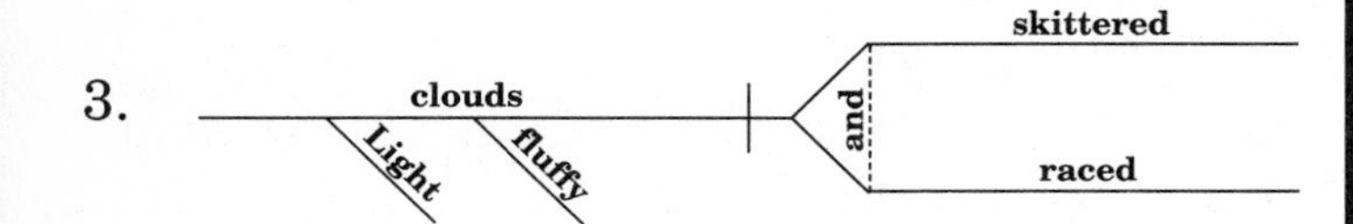

4.

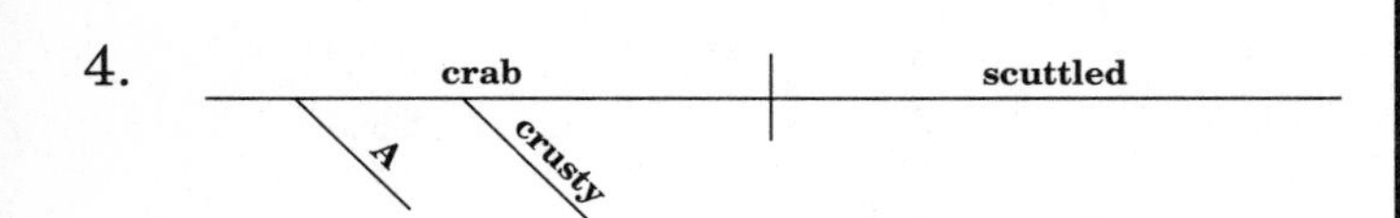

5.

drink | would help
A
cool

6.

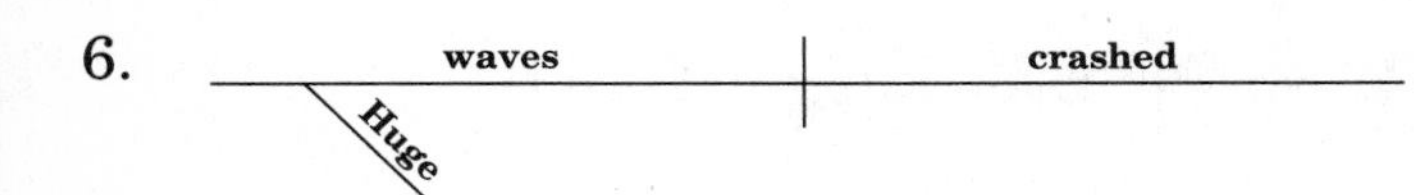

7.

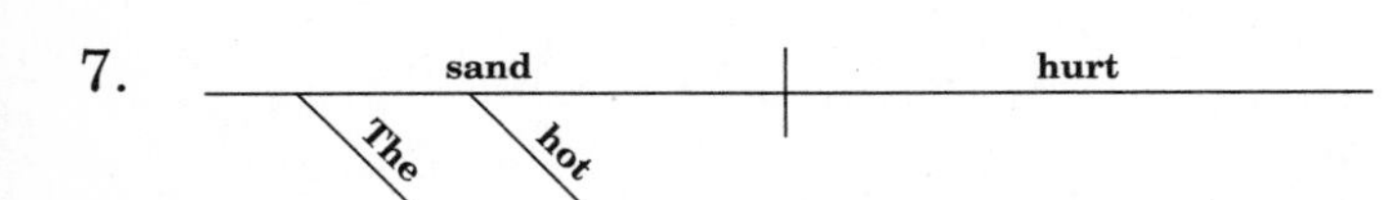

8.

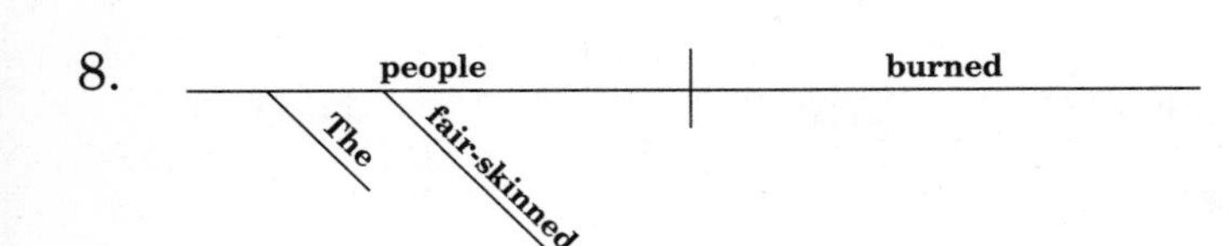

9.

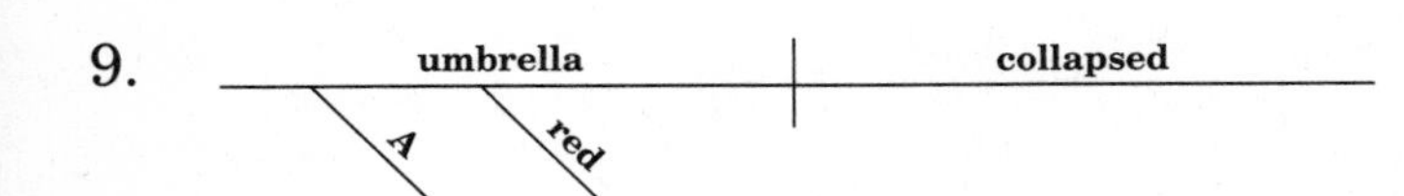

10.

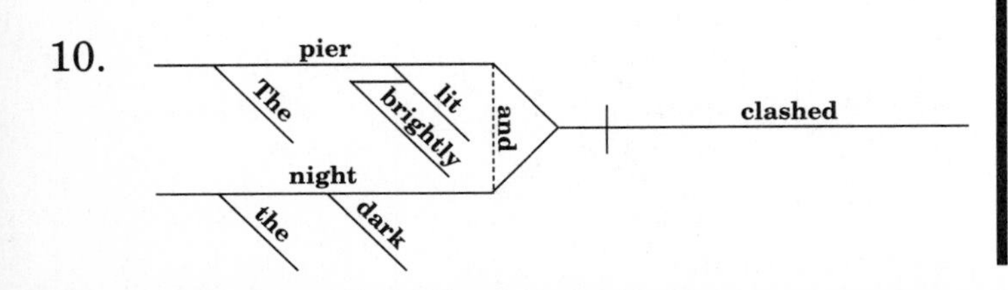

EXERCISE 2 — page 8 (Answers will vary)

EXERCISE 3 — page 9

1.

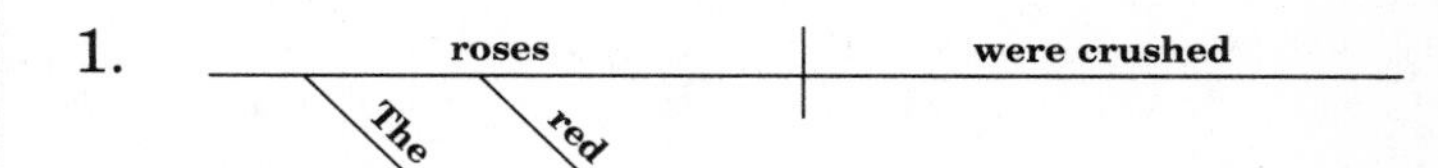

2.

violets | bloomed
The
purple

3.

car | will race
The
flashy
new
silver

4.

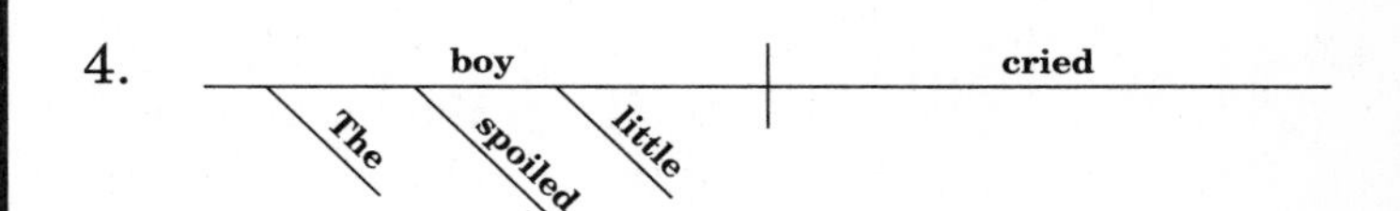

5.

bull | charged
The
raging

EXERCISE 4 — page 9

1.

tank | can break
A
glass
fish

2.

kite | soared
The
big
blue

3.

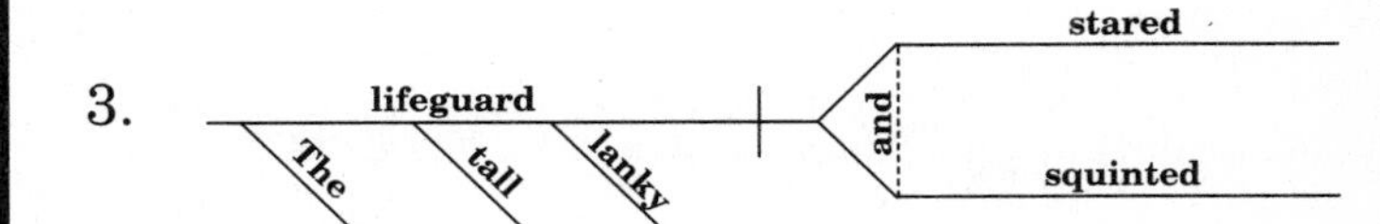

4.

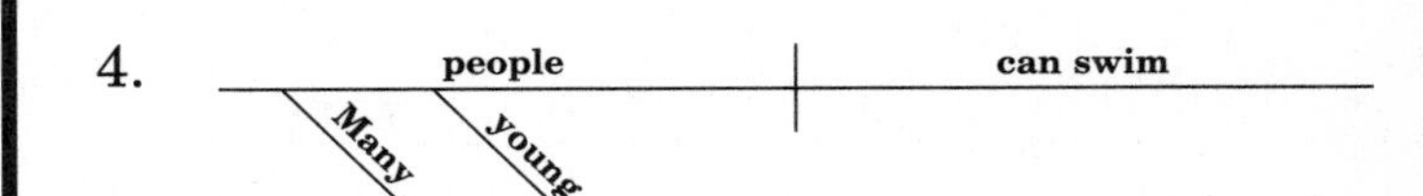

5.

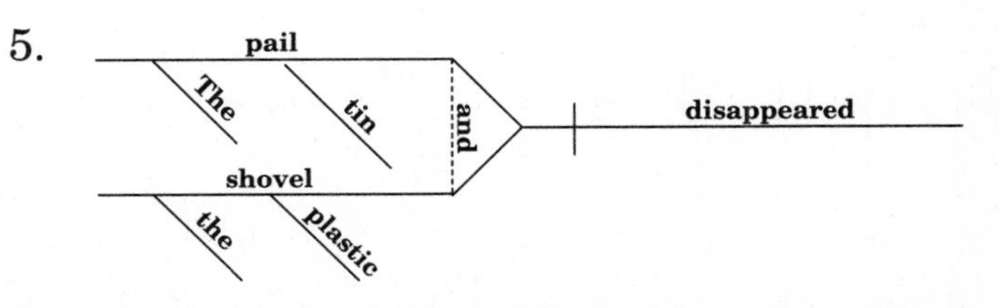

Answer Key

EXERCISE 1 — page 10

1.
flame | burned
The, gas, brightly

2.
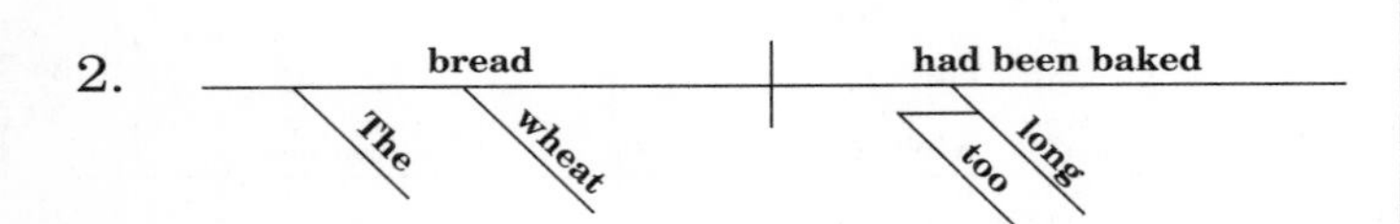

3.
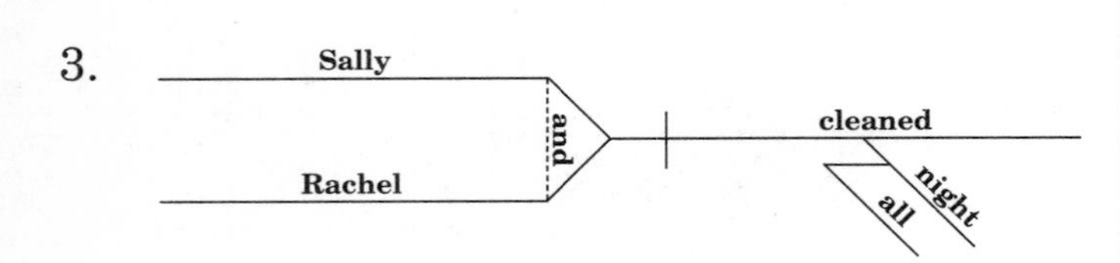

4.
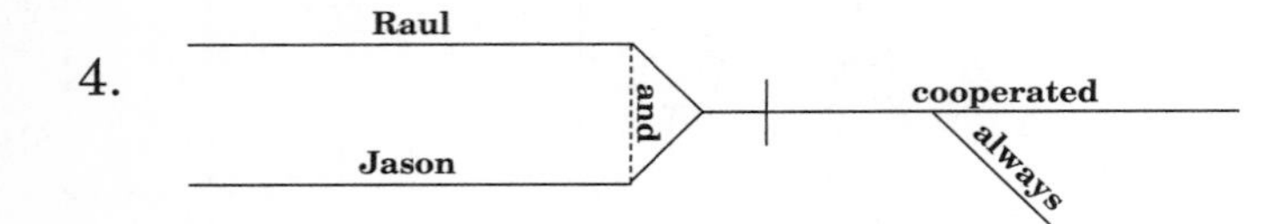

5.
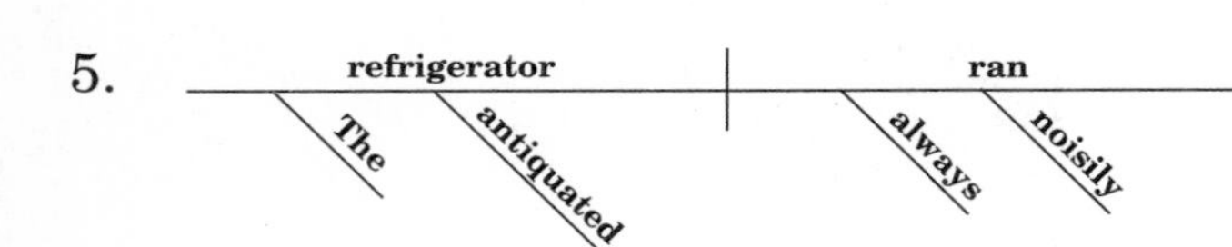

6.
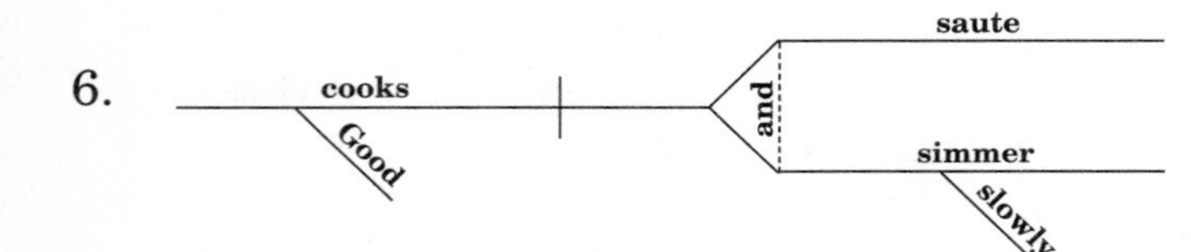

7.
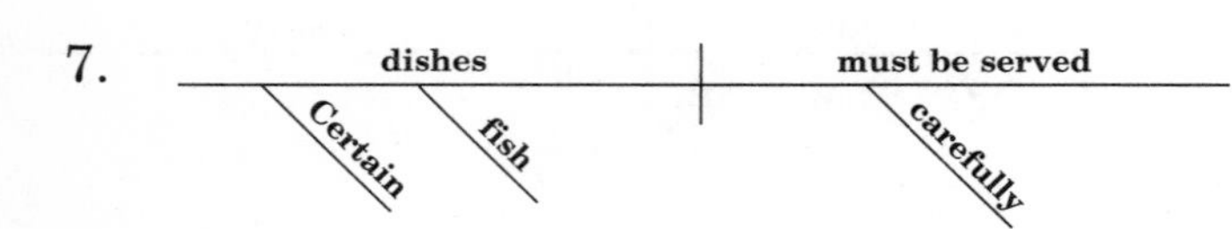

8.
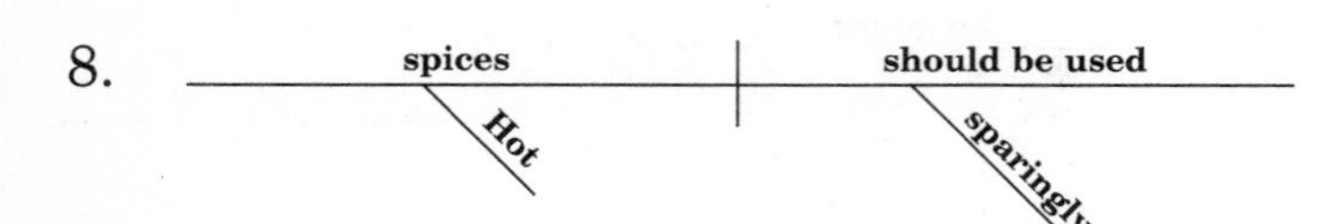

9.
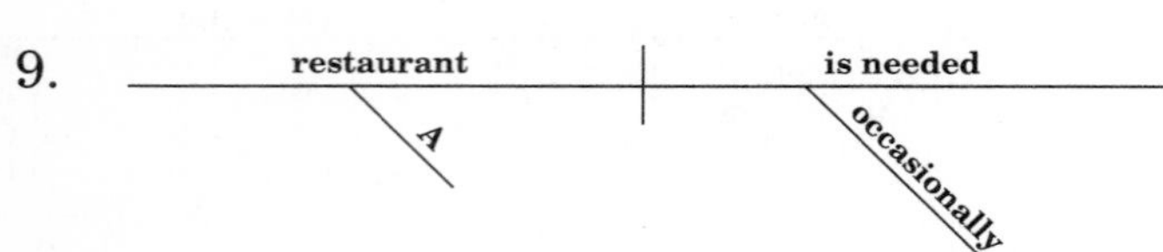

10.
recipe | must be followed
A, complicated, exactly

EXERCISE 2 — page 10 (Answers will vary)

EXERCISE 3 — page 11

1.
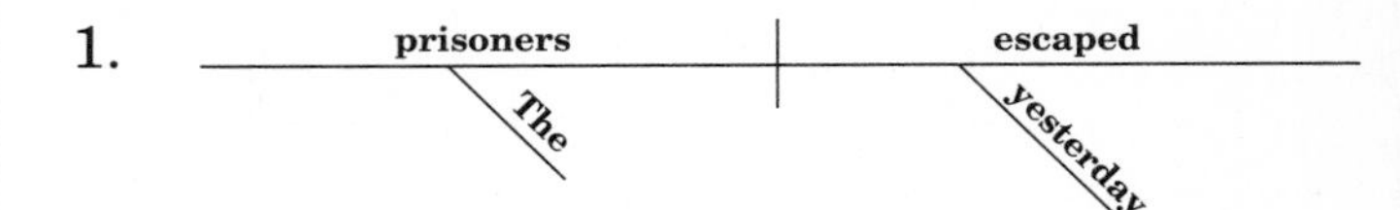

2.
refugees | were returned
The, immediately

3.
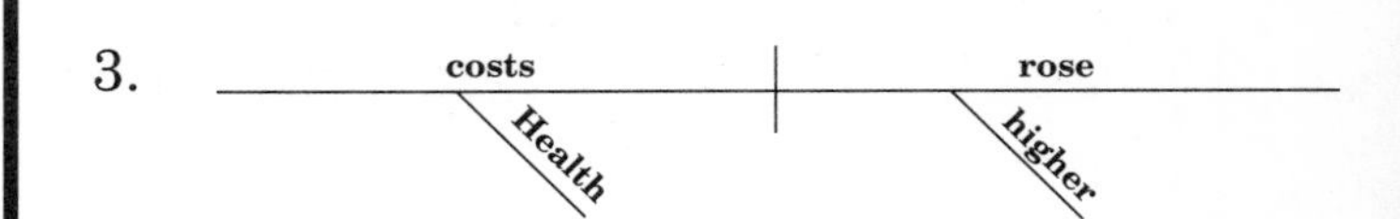

4.
team | will play
The, tonight

5.
ball | was served
The, wide

EXERCISE 4 — page 11

1.
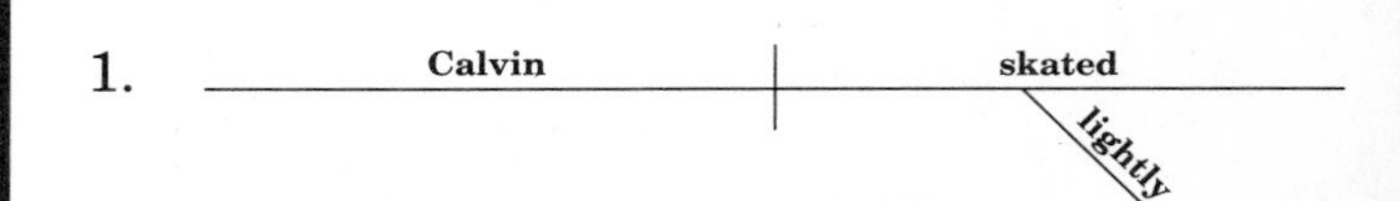

2.
sauce | splattered
The, wildly

3.
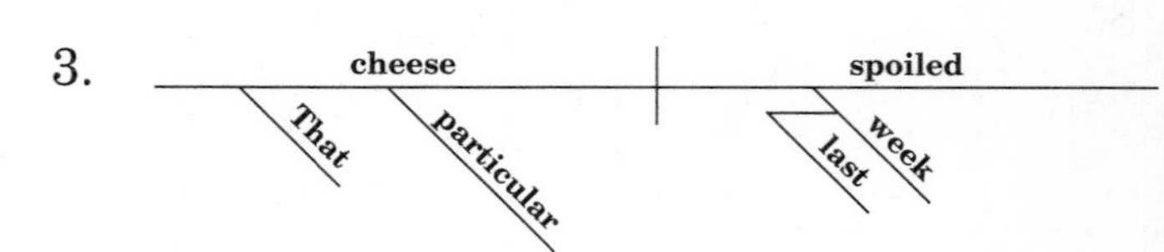

4.
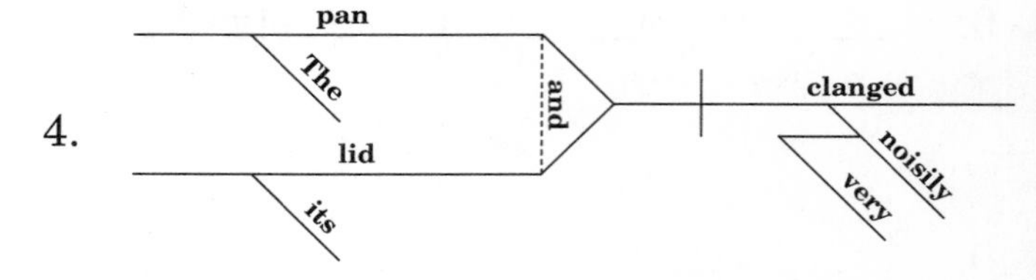

5.
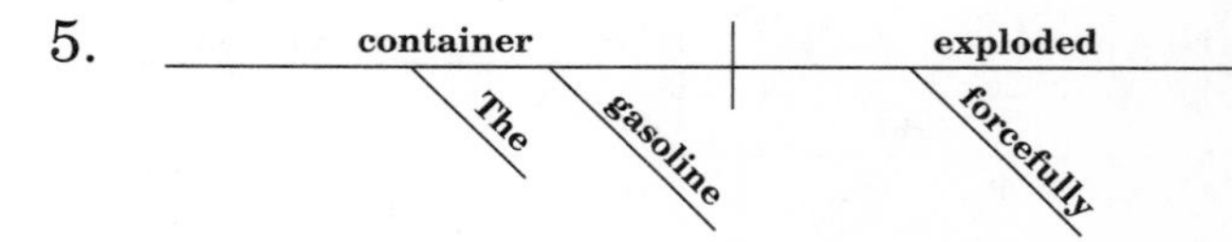

Answer Key

EXERCISE 1 — page 12

1. Kerry (sister) | left
my, older | immediately

2. 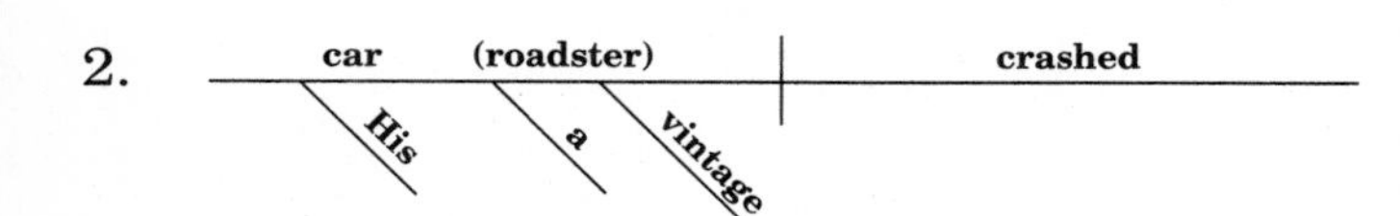

3. 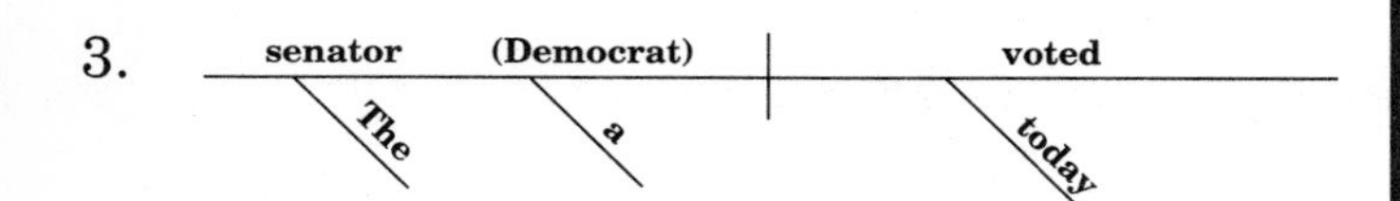

4. 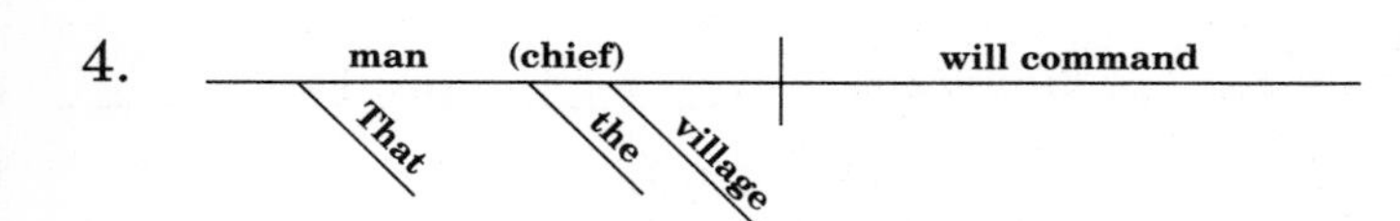

5. 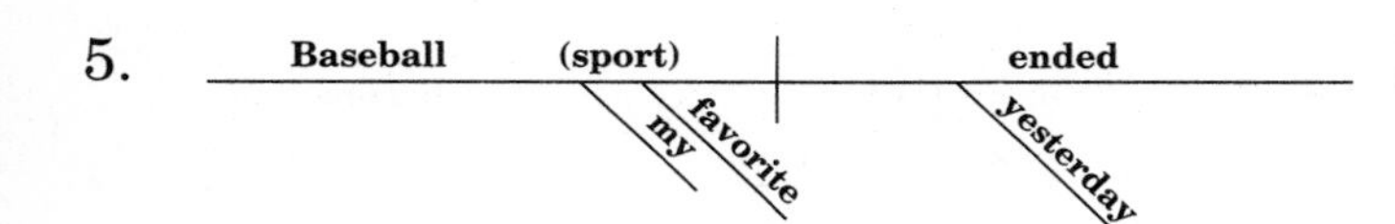

6. 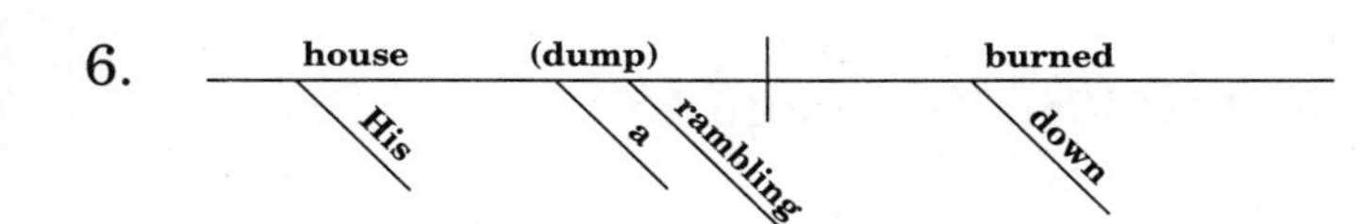

7. 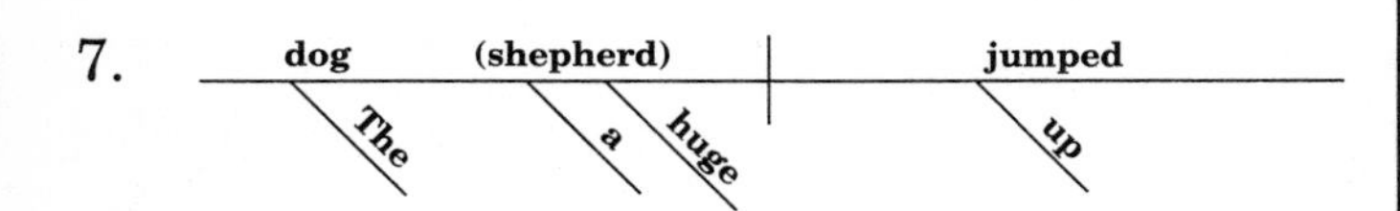

8. 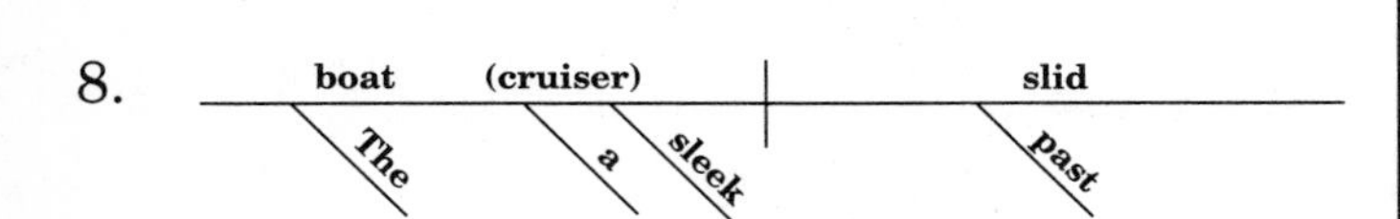

9. 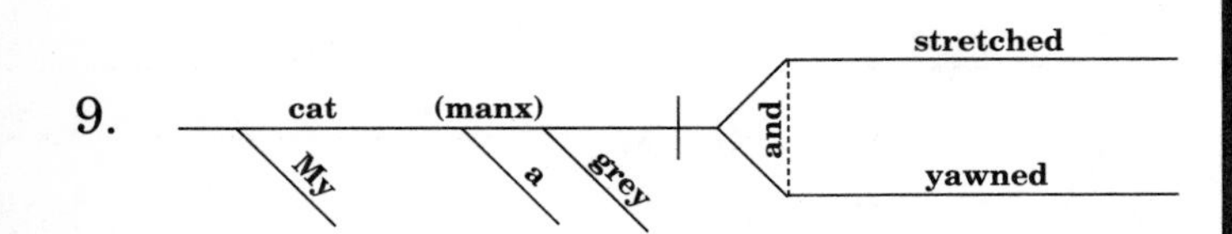

10. 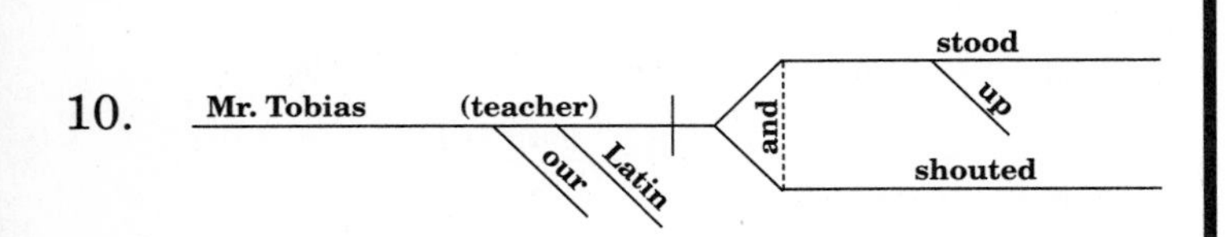

EXERCISE 2 — page 12 (Answers will vary)

EXERCISE 3, PAGE 13

1. 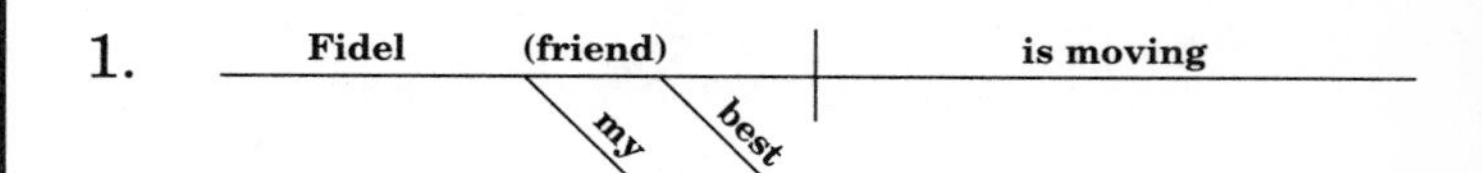

2. catcher (player) | is batting
The, their, best | next

3. Batman (crime fighter) | jumped
a, real | down

4. 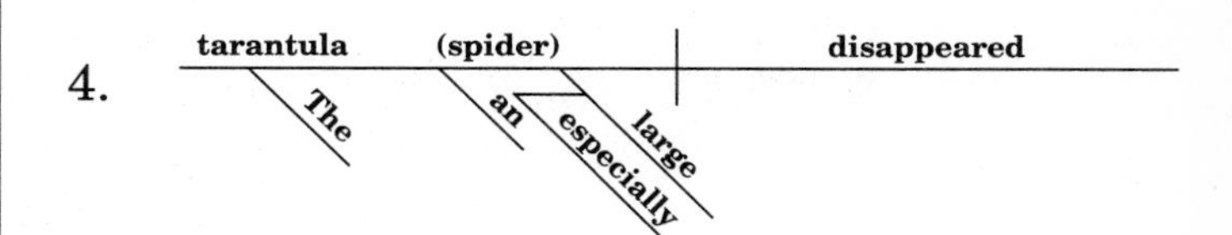

5. Horace (student) | won
an, all, "A"

EXERCISE 4 — page 13

1. Terri Travis (chairman) | officiated
the

2. Tiko Tanaka (mailman) | passed
our | by

3. dog (runt) | was pushed
My, the | down

4. girl (student) | will graduate
The, new, a, very, good | tomorrow

5. 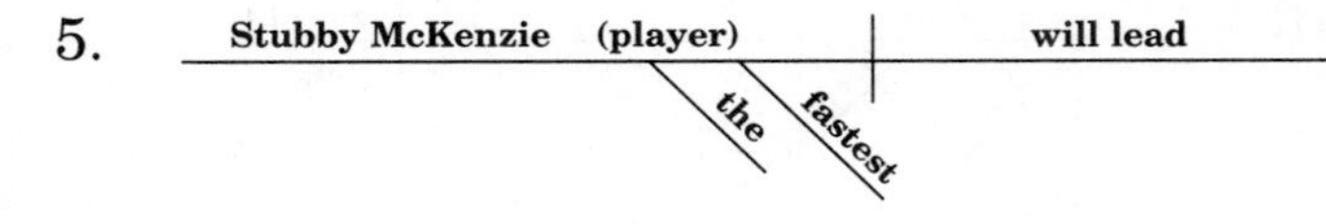

Answer Key

EXERCISE 1 — page 14

1.

friend
is leaving
My
with
arm
the
broken

2. 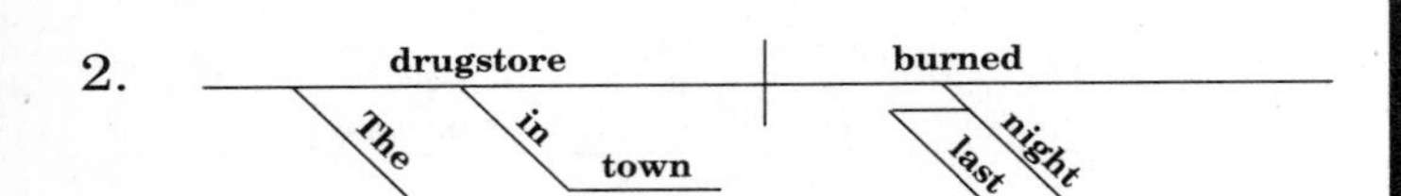

3. 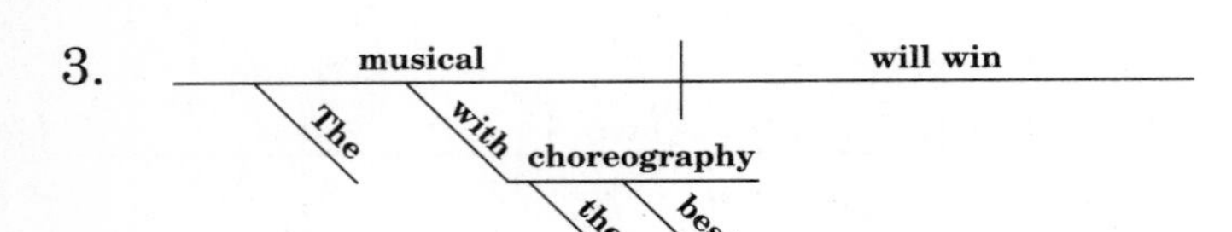

4. 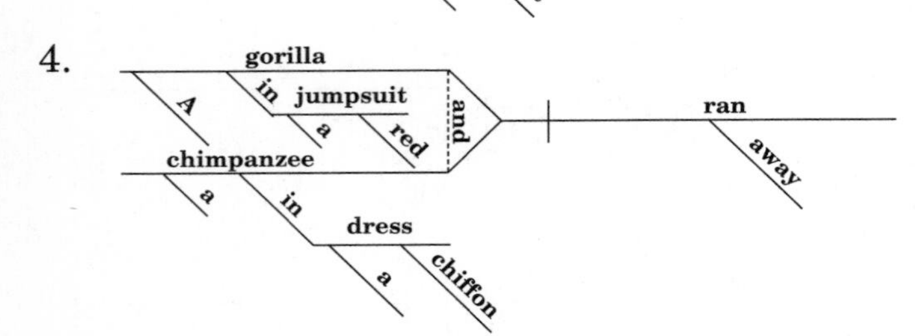

5. 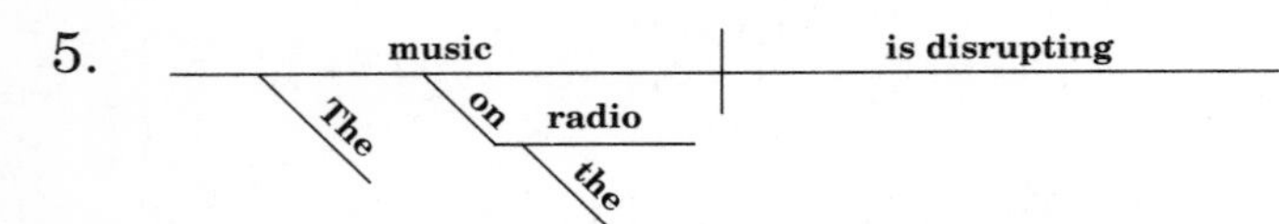

6. 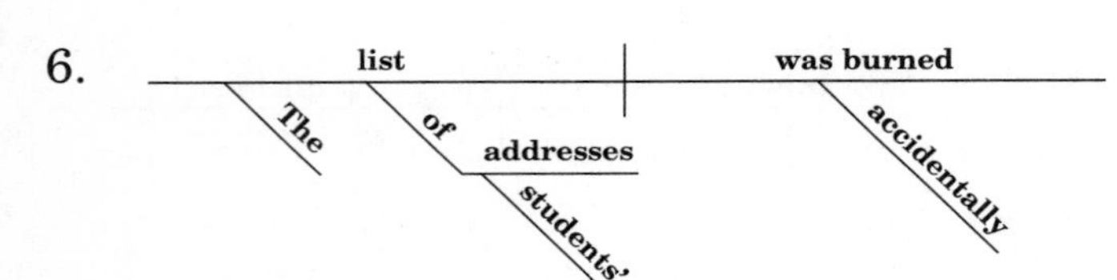

7. 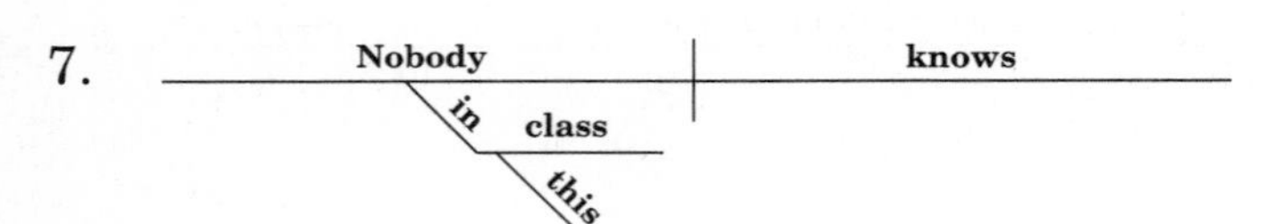

8. 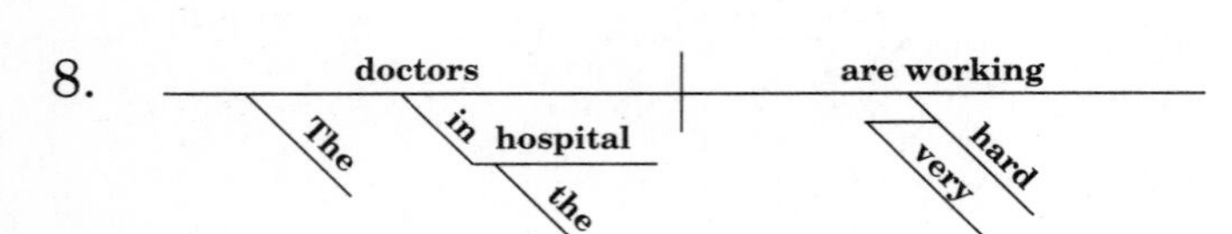

9. 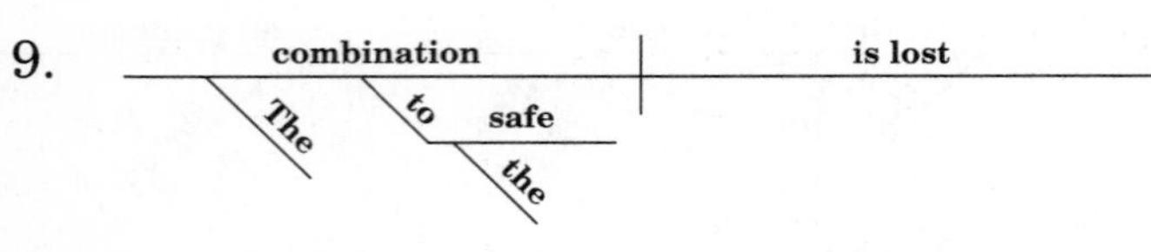

10. 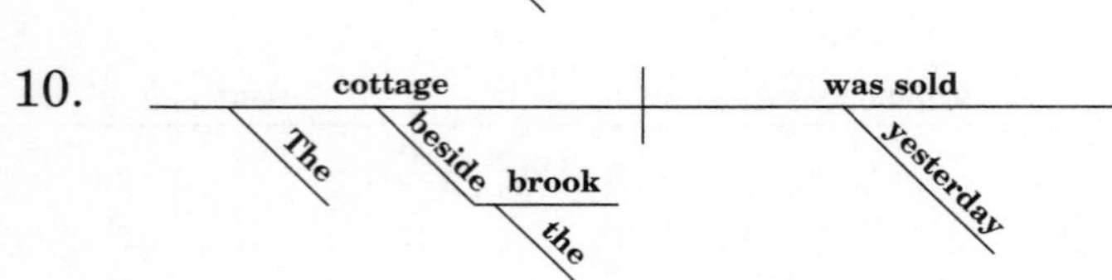

EXERCISE 2 — page 14 (Answers will vary)

EXERCISE 3 — page 15

1. 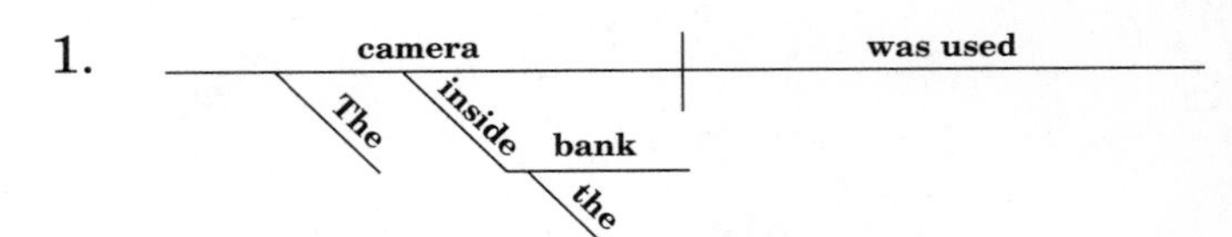

2. 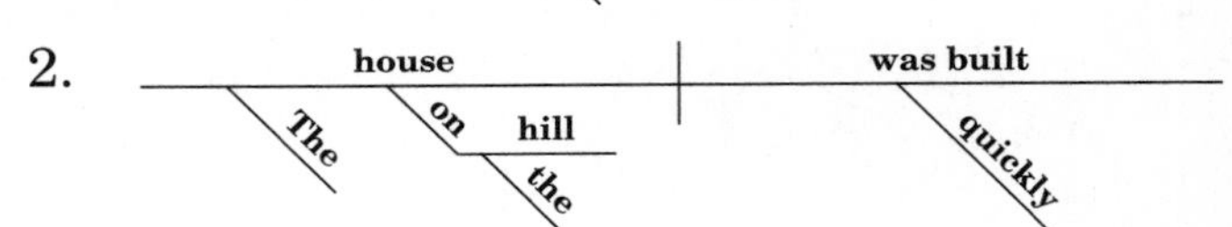

3. 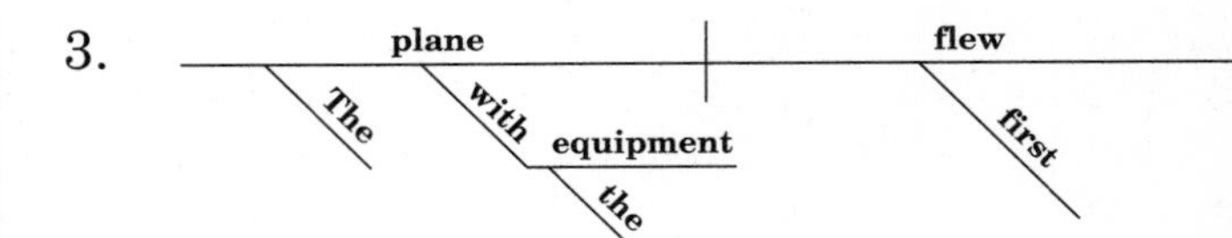

4. 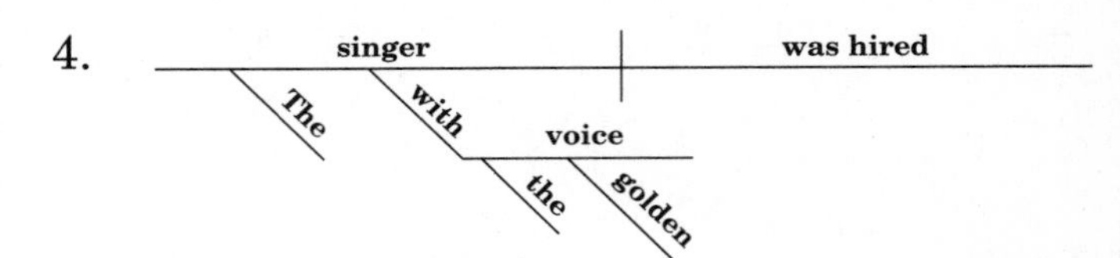

5. 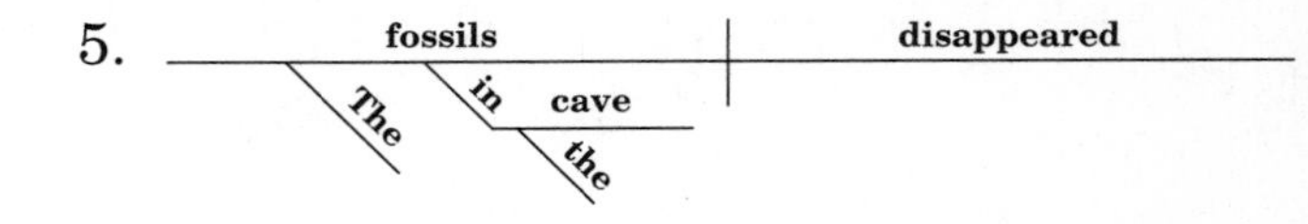

EXERCISE 4 — page 15

1. 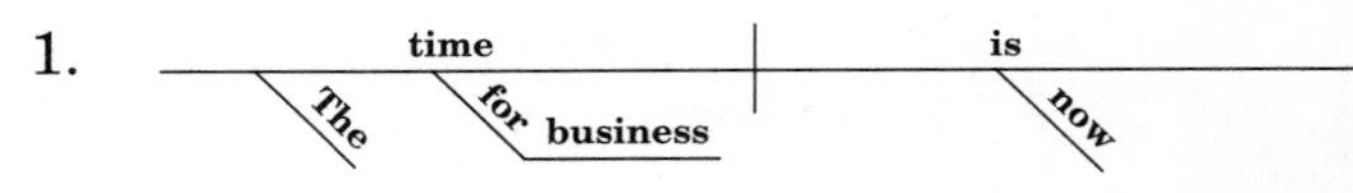

2. 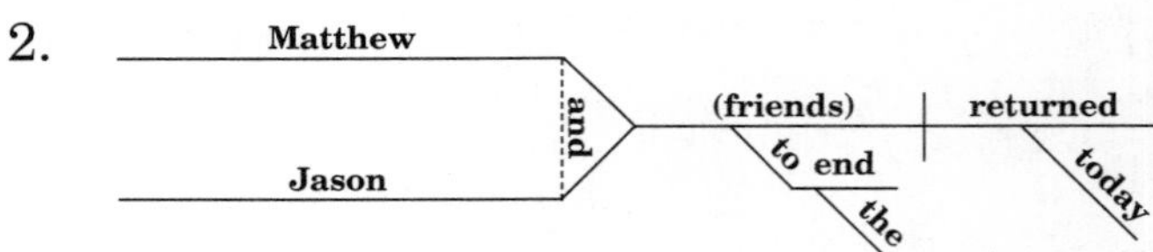

3. 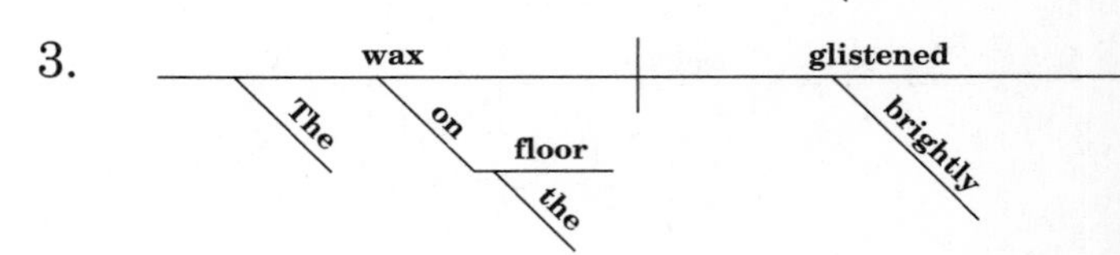

4. 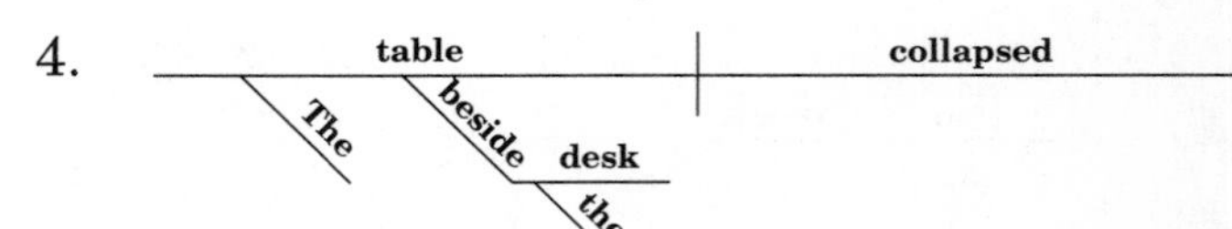

5. 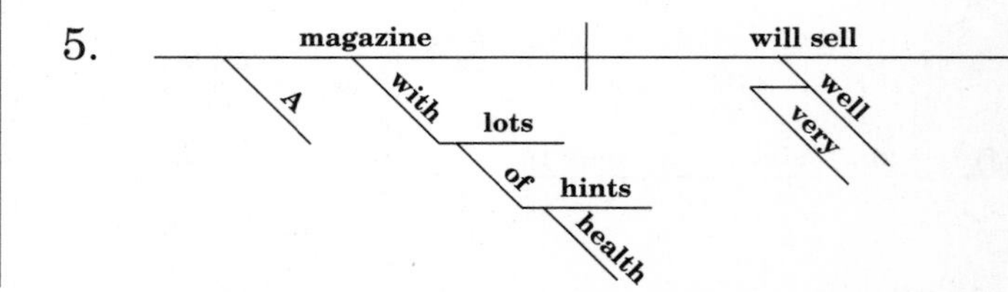

Answer Key

EXERCISE 1 — page 16

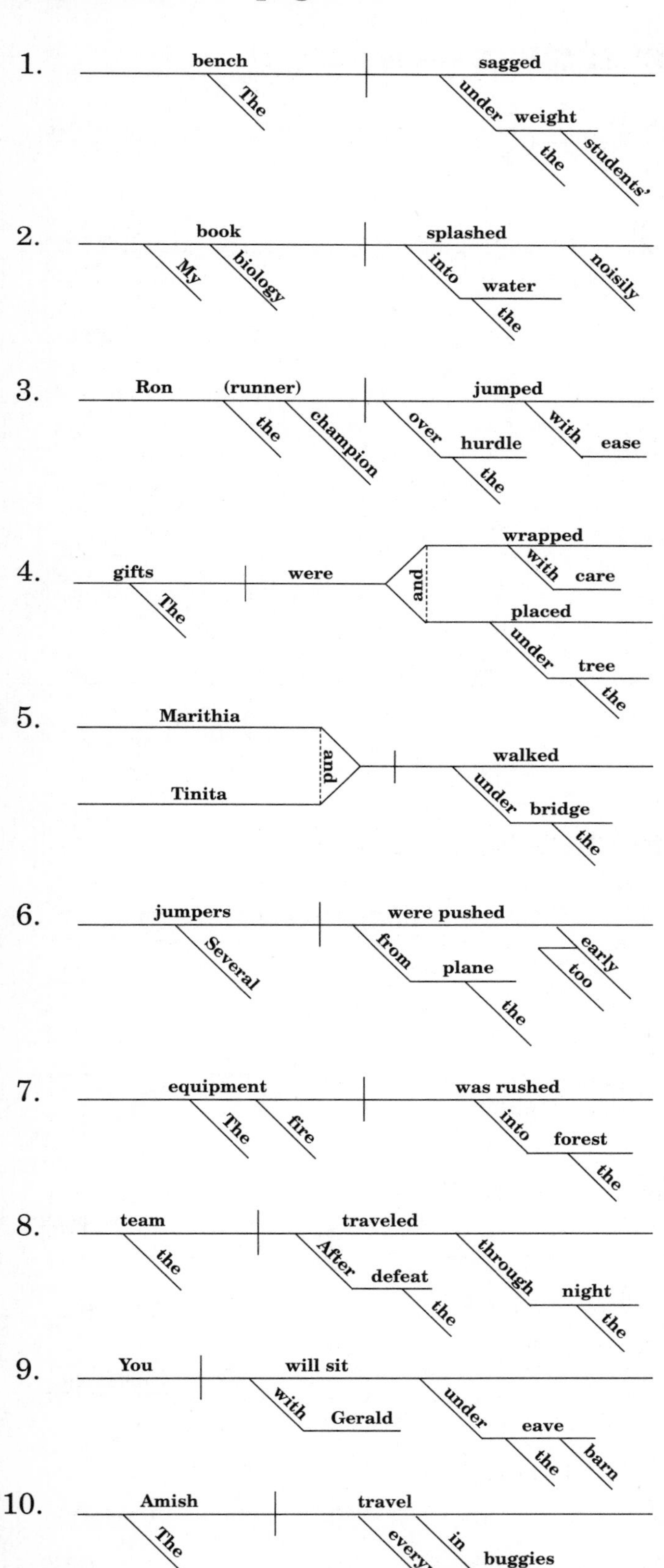

EXERCISE 2 — page 16 (Answers will vary)

EXERCISE 3 — page 17

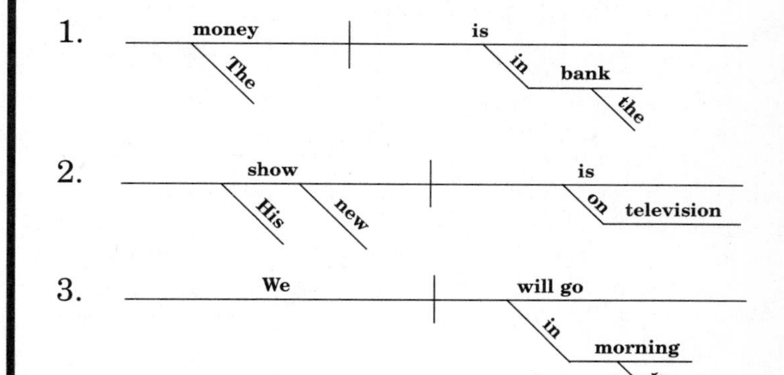

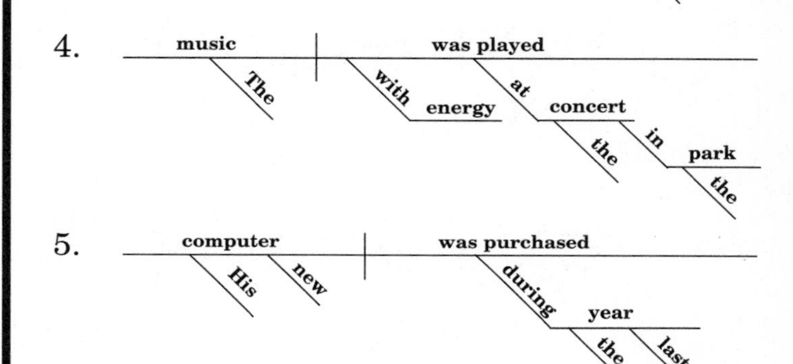

EXERCISE 4 — page 17

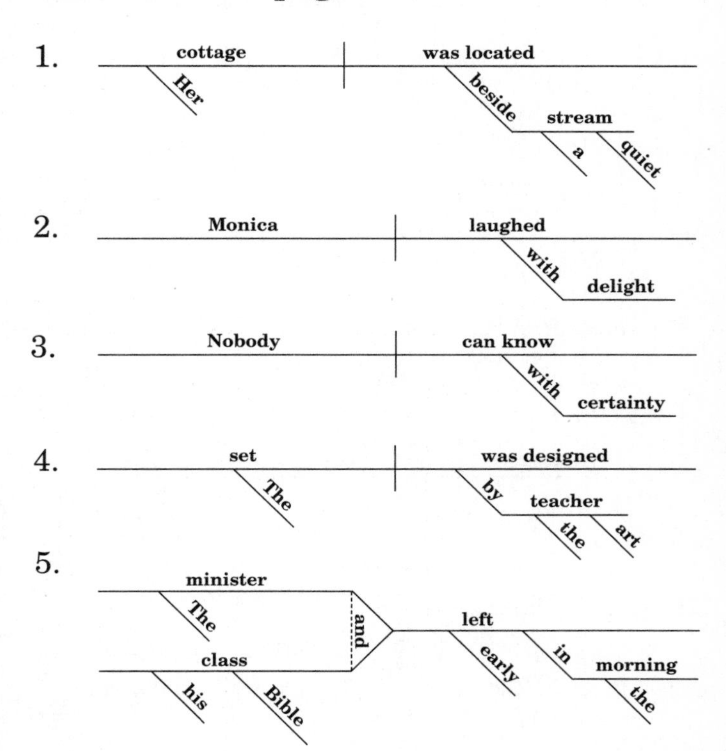

Answer Key

EXERCISE 1 — page 18

1.
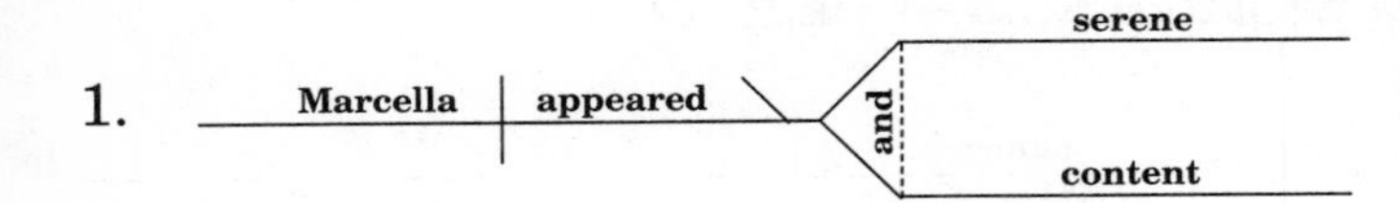

2.
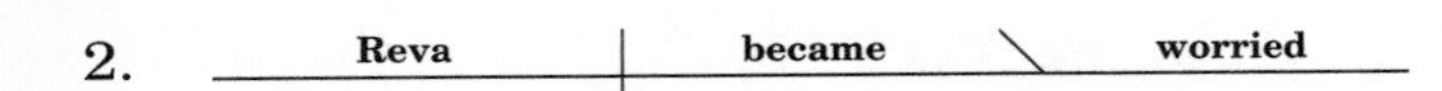

3.
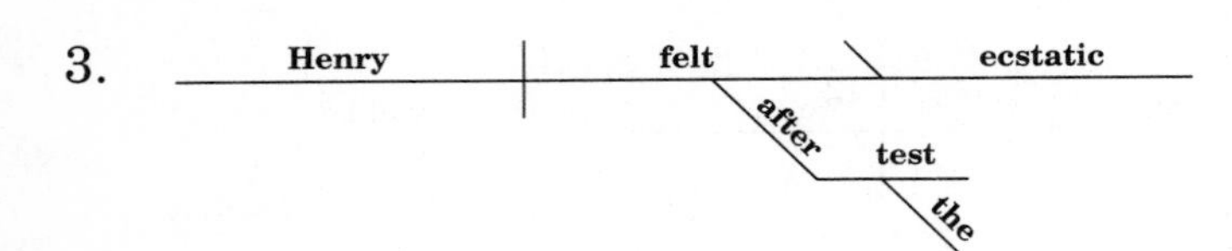

4.
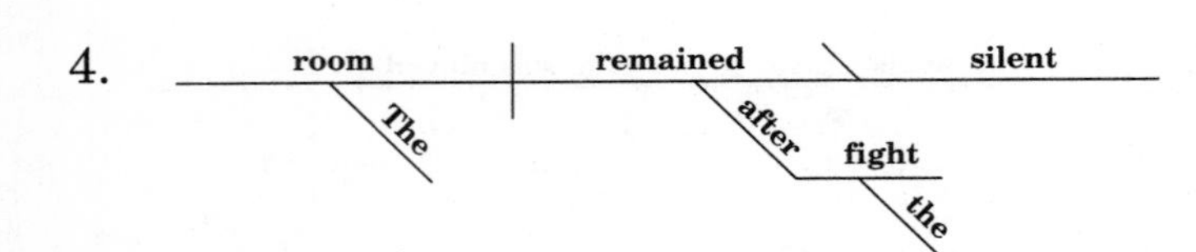

5.
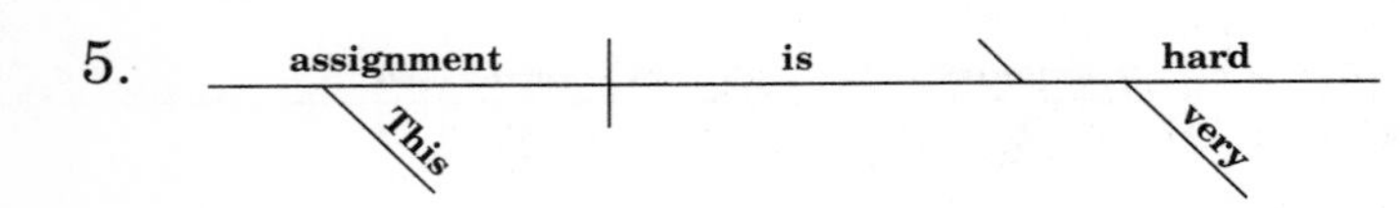

6.
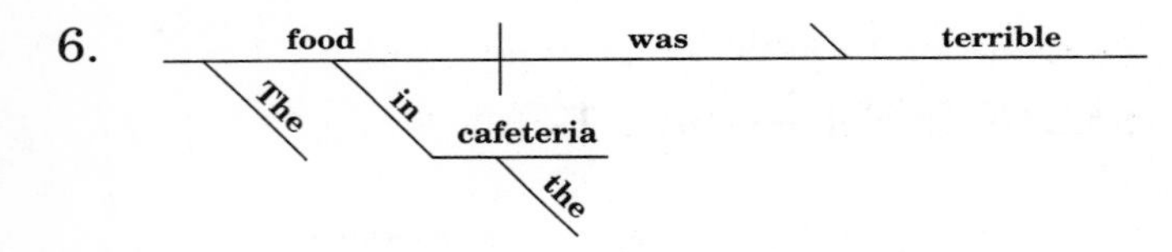

7.
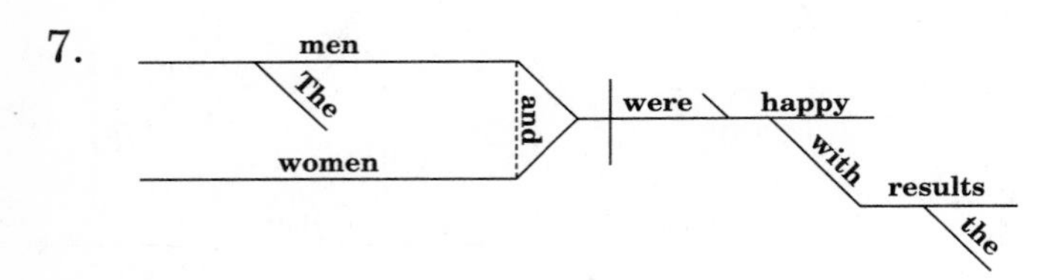

8.
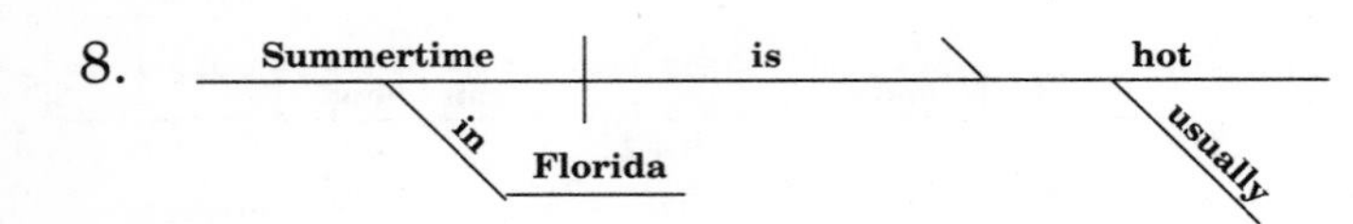

9.
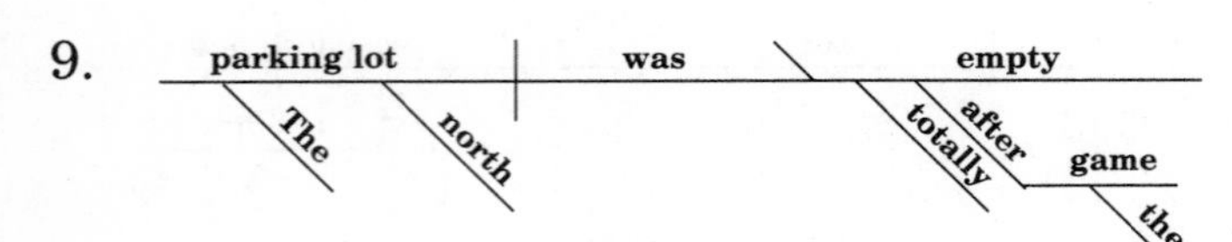

10.
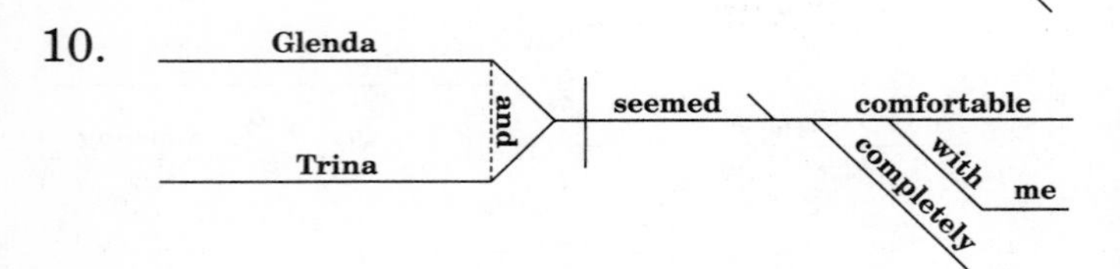

EXERCISE 2 — page 18 (Answers will vary)

EXERCISE 3 — page 19

1.
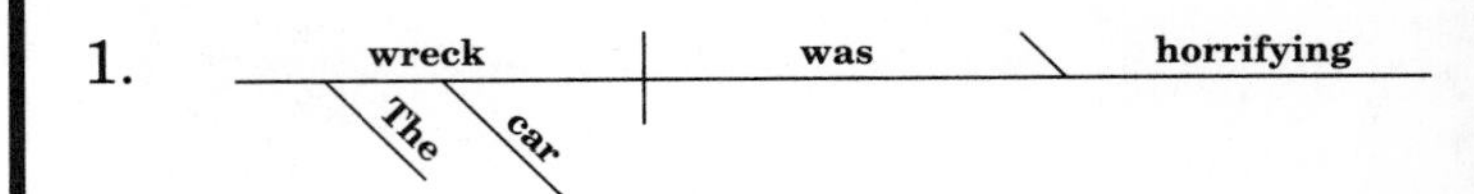

2. She | looked \ marvelous

3.
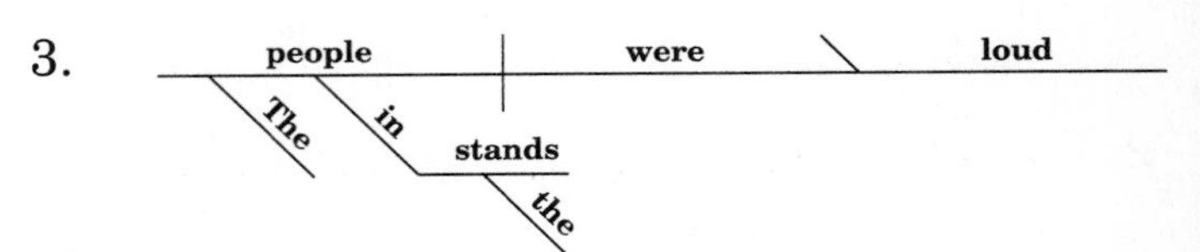

4.
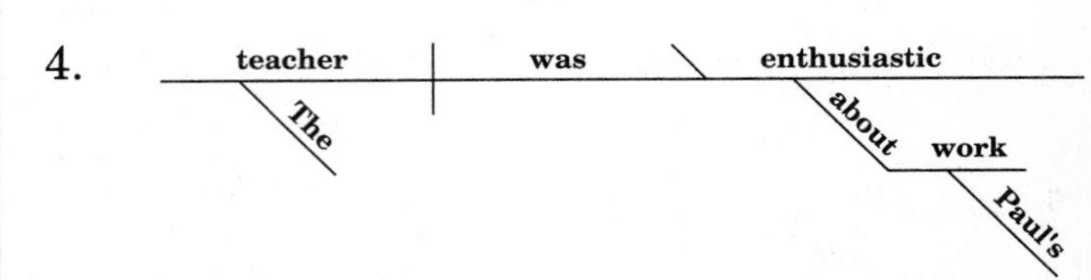

5.
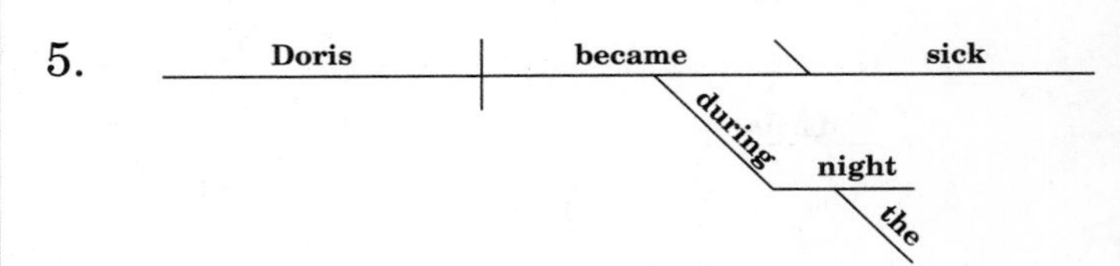

EXERCISE 4 — page 19

1.–2.
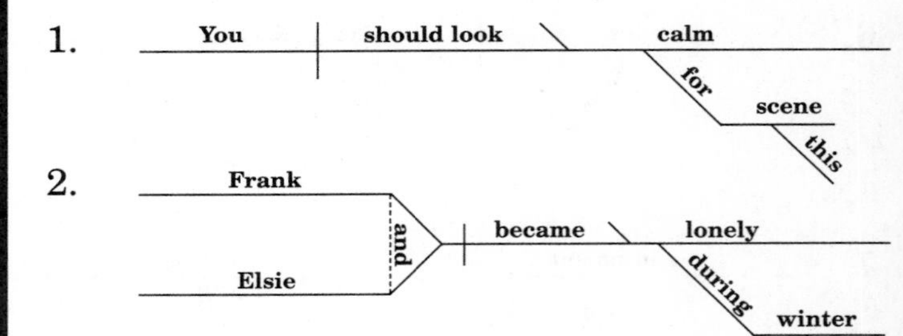

3.–4.
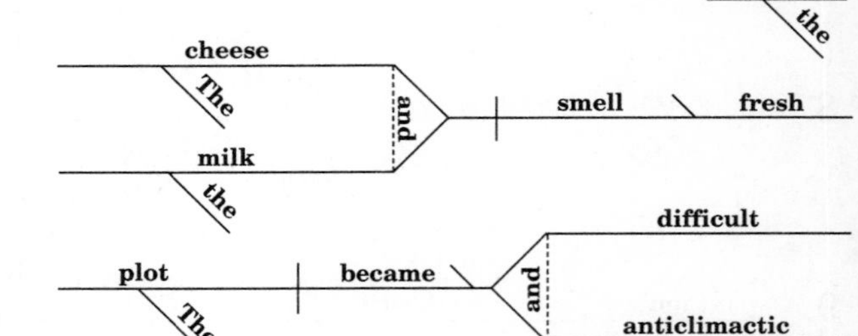

5.
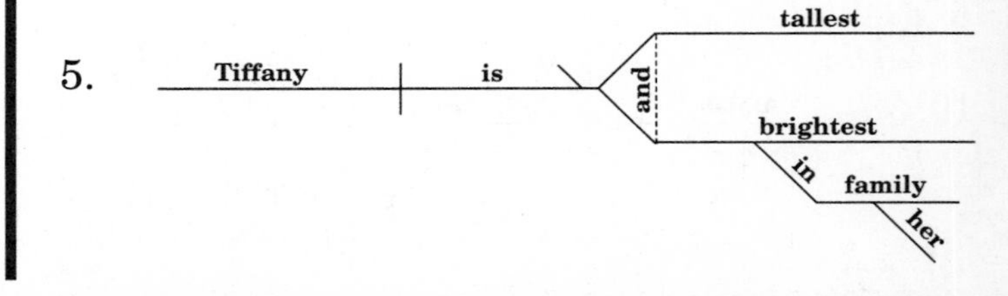

Answer Key

EXERCISE 1 — page 20

1. Mark | became \ consultant — after retirement — his — a

2. 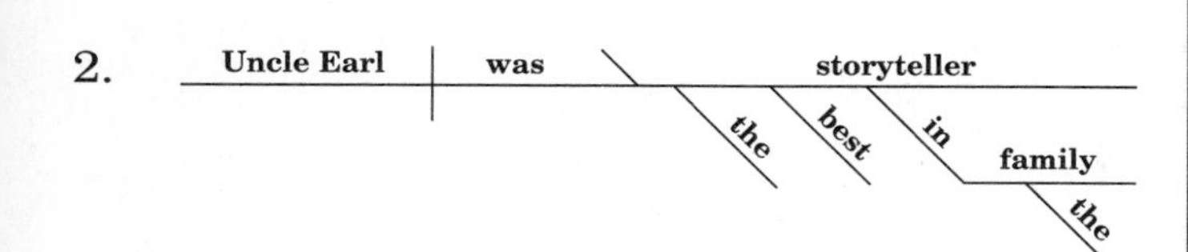

3. 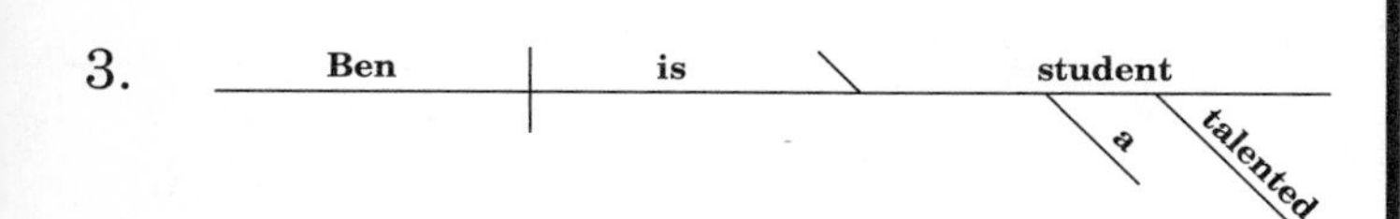

4. 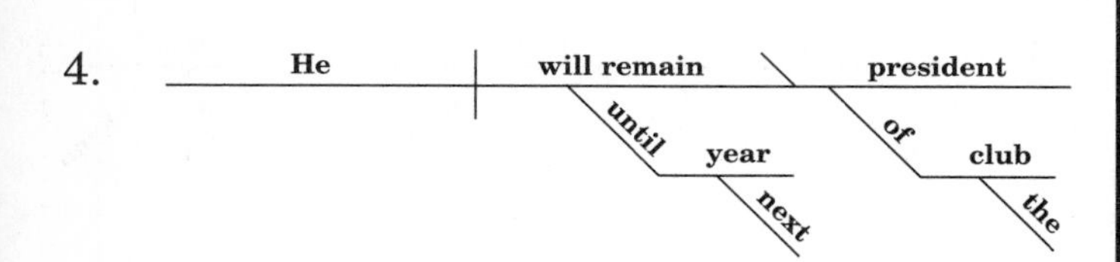

5. 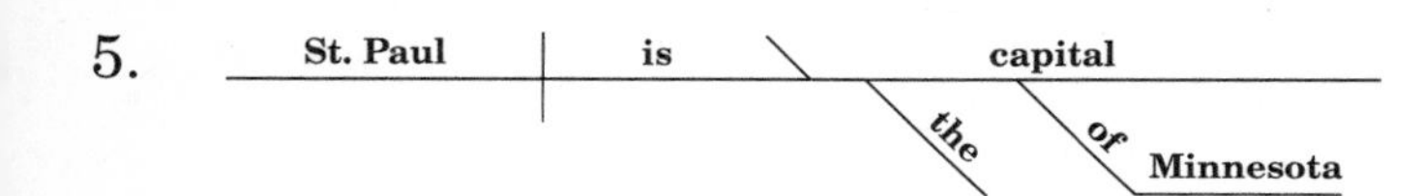

6. 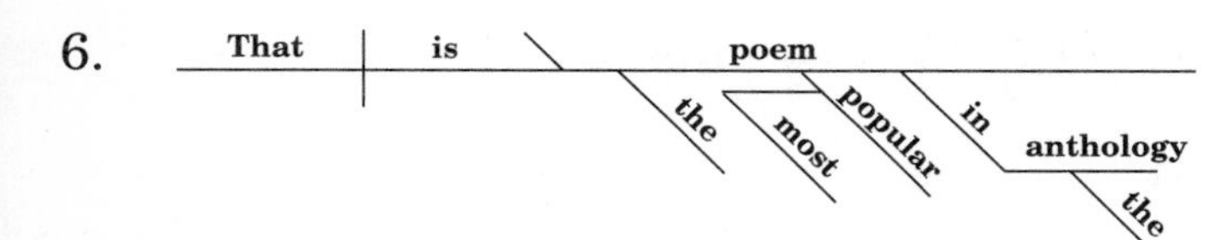

7. 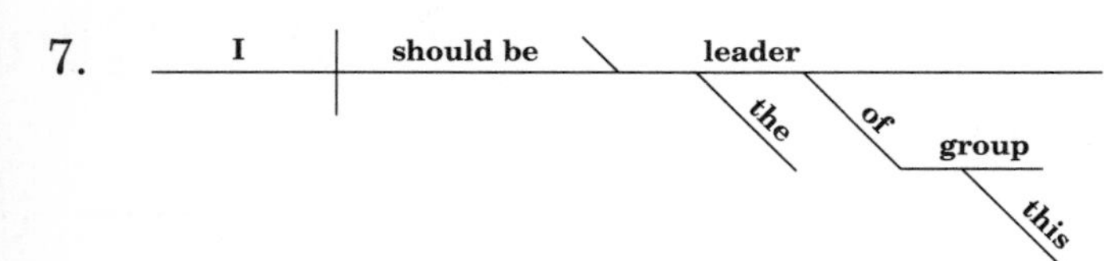

8. 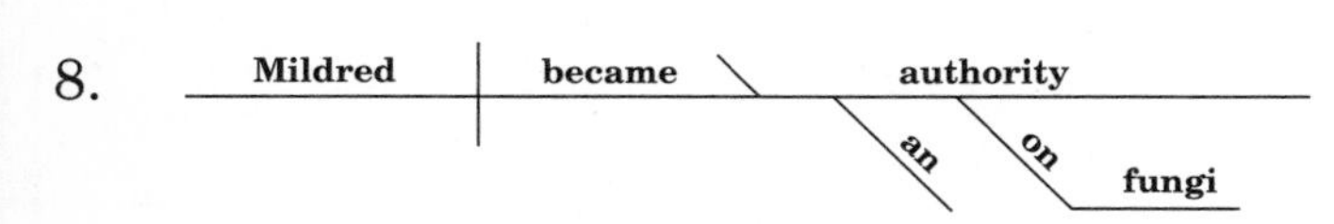

9. 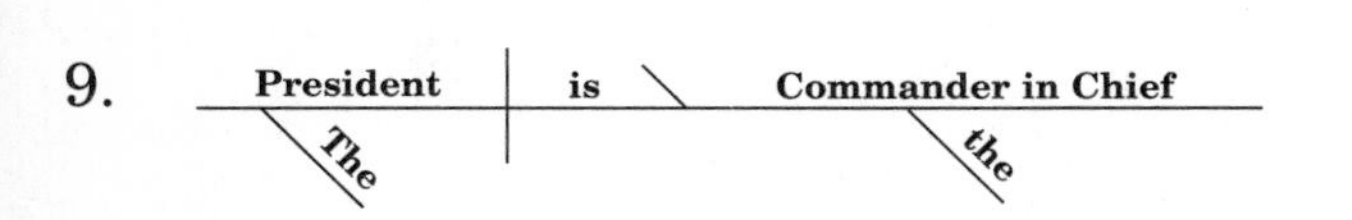

10. Alaska | became \ part — in century — this — of United States — the

EXERCISE 2 — page 20 (Answers will vary)

EXERCISE 3 — page 21

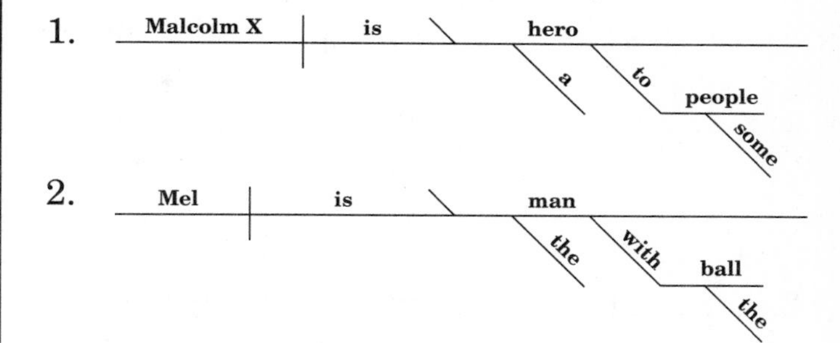

3. 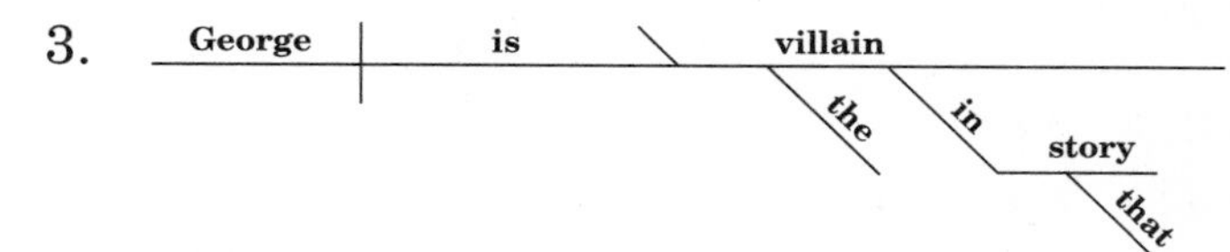

4. 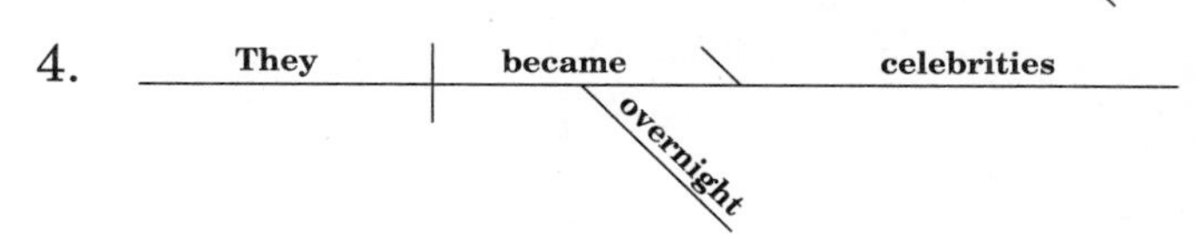

5. Warren Spahn | was \ pitcher — a — great

EXERCISE 4 — page 21

1. 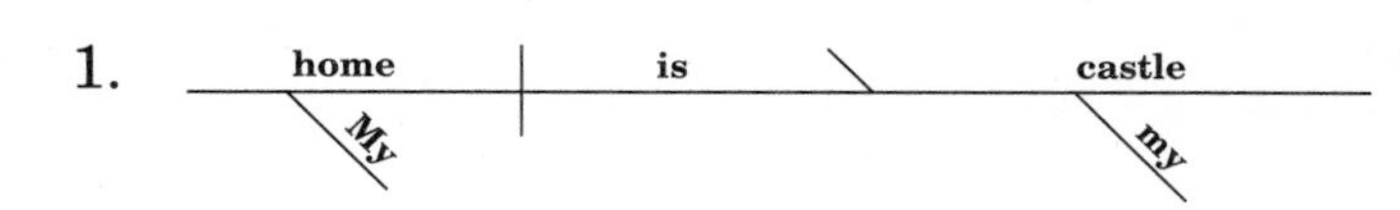

2. Michigan | is \ state — my — favorite

3. He | was appointed \ treasurer

4. 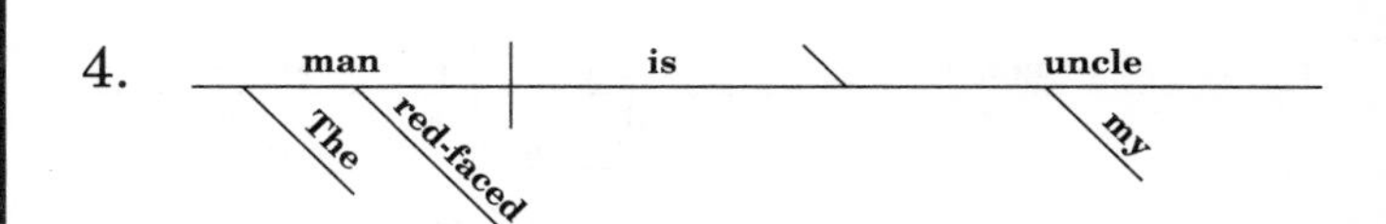

5. 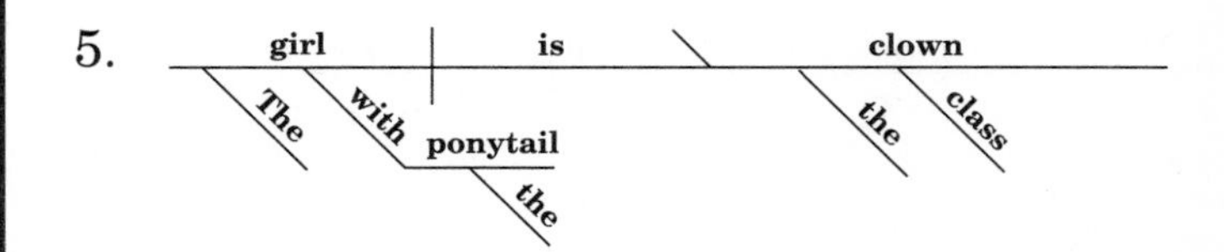

Answer Key

EXERCISE 1 — page 22

1. 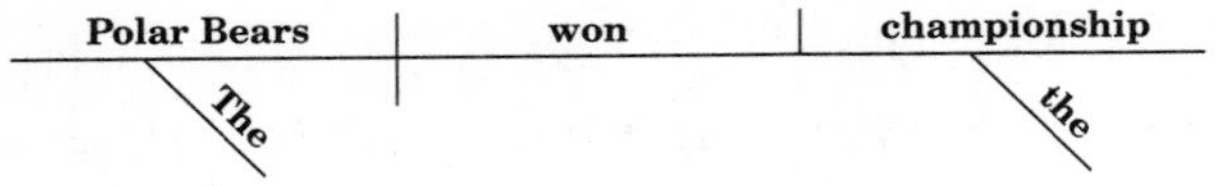 Polar Bears | won | championship; The; the

2. 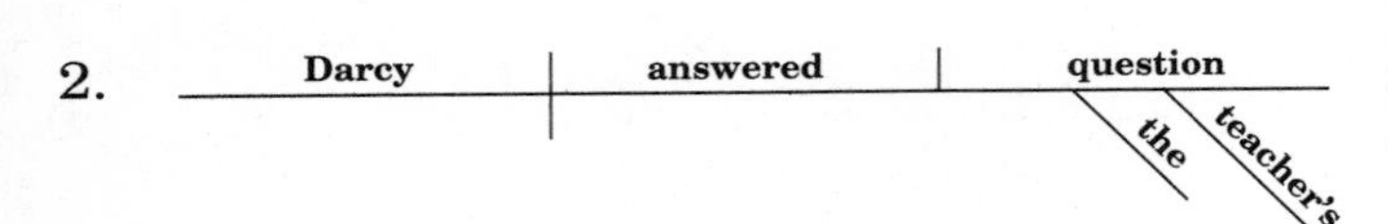

3. 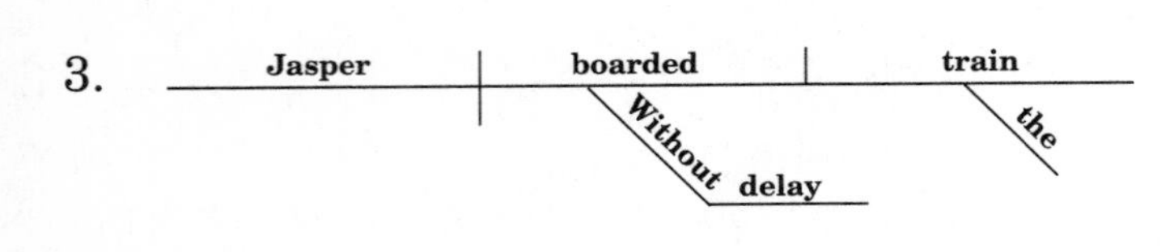

4. 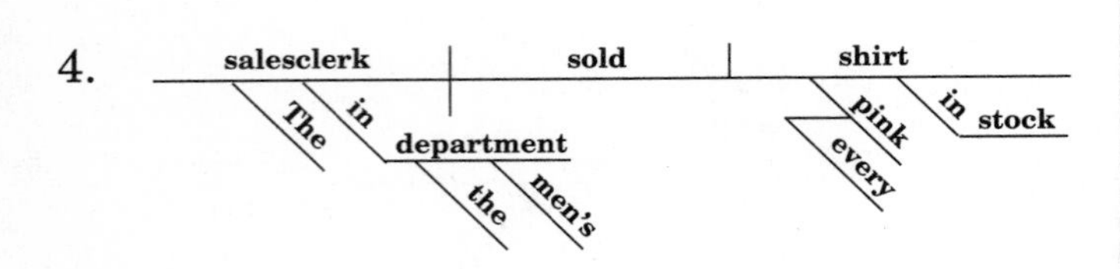

5. 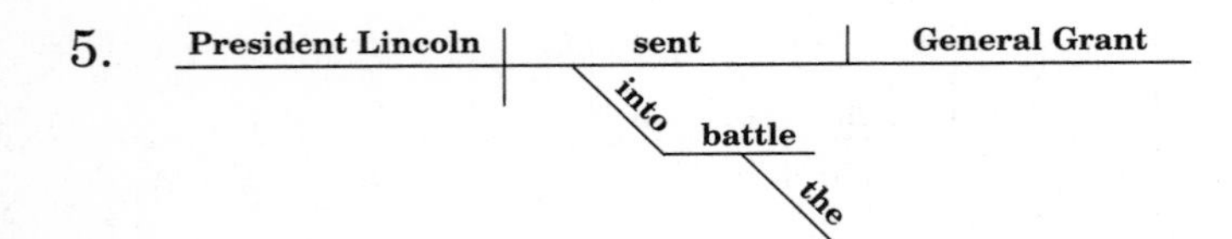

6. 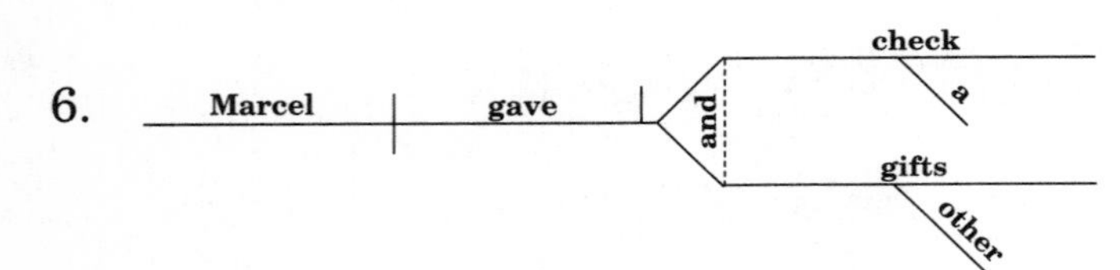

7. 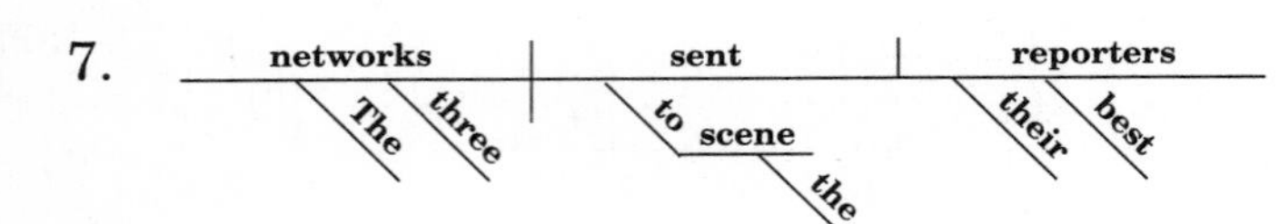

8. 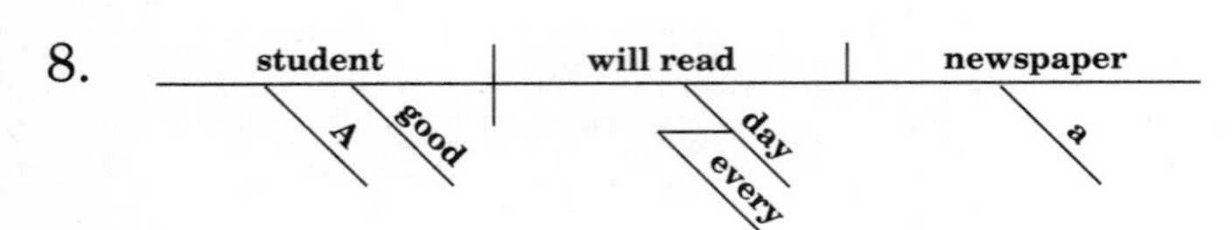

9. 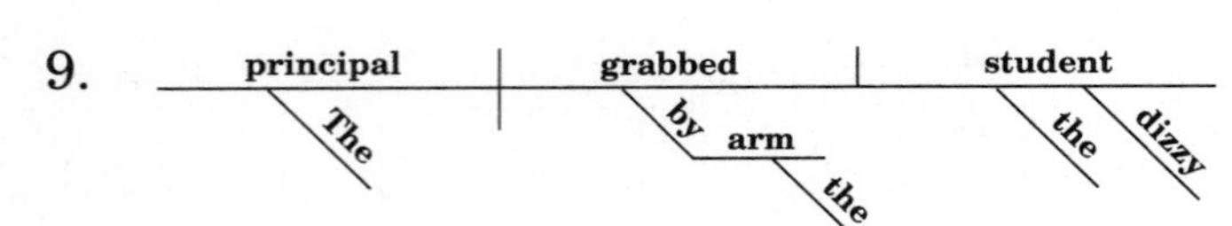

10. 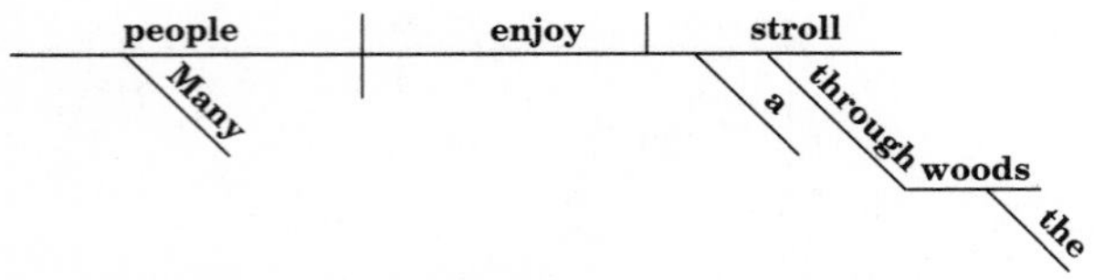 people | enjoy | stroll; Many; a; through woods; the

EXERCISE 2 — page 22 (Answers will vary)

EXERCISE 3 — page 23

1. 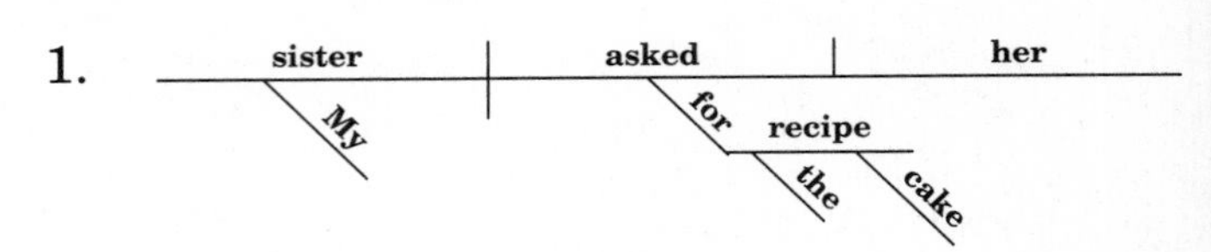

2. 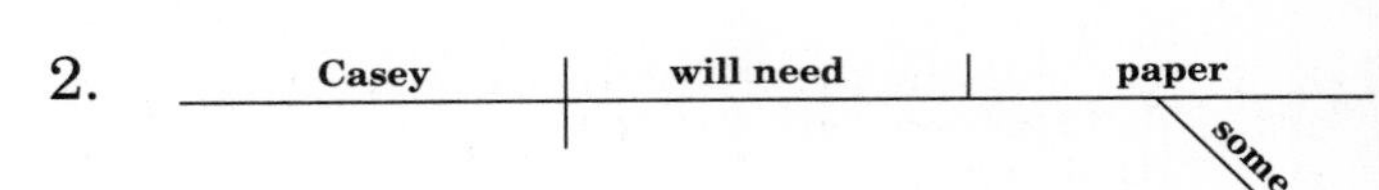

3. 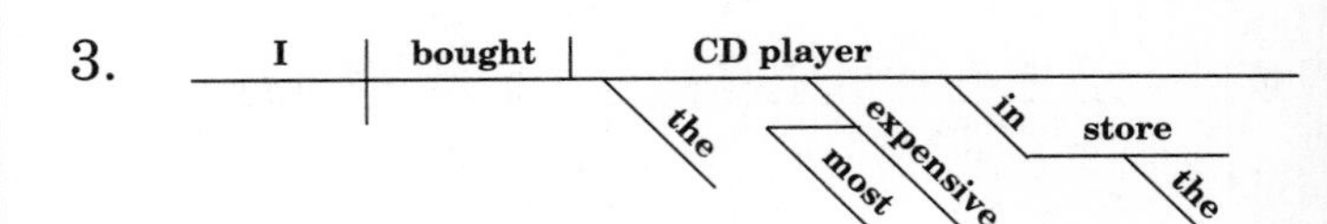

4. 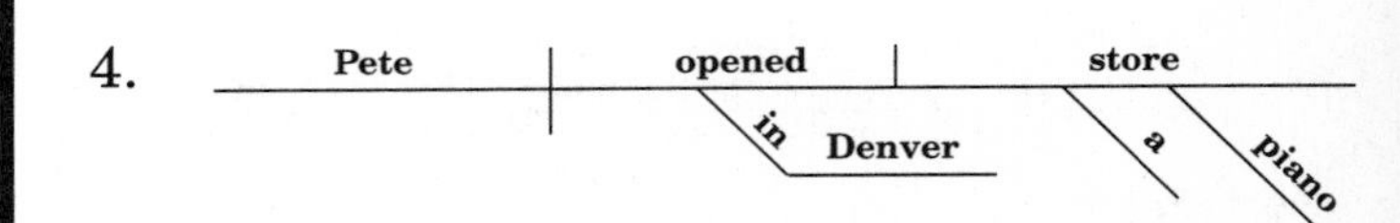

5. 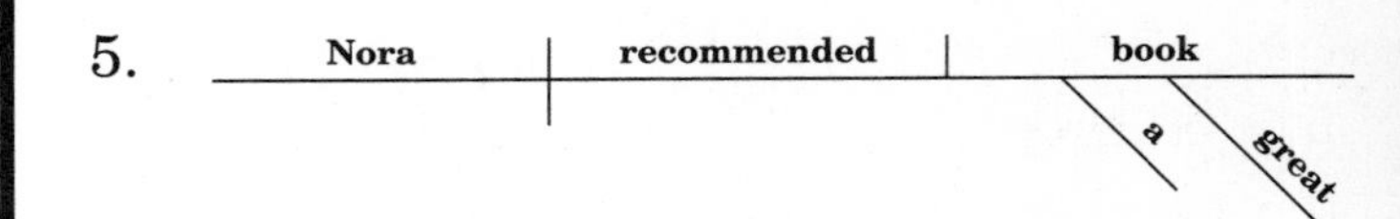

EXERCISE 4 — page 23

1. 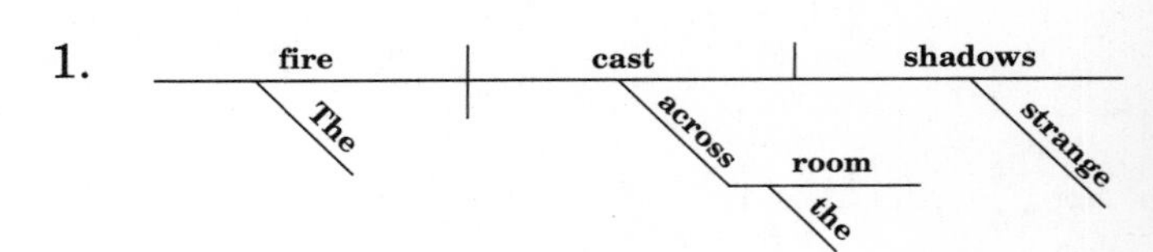

2. 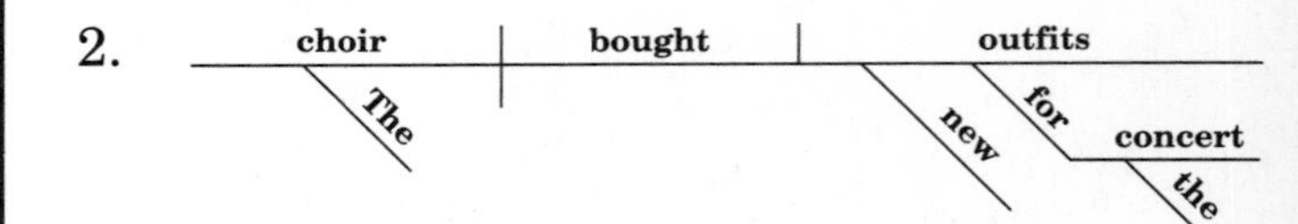

3. 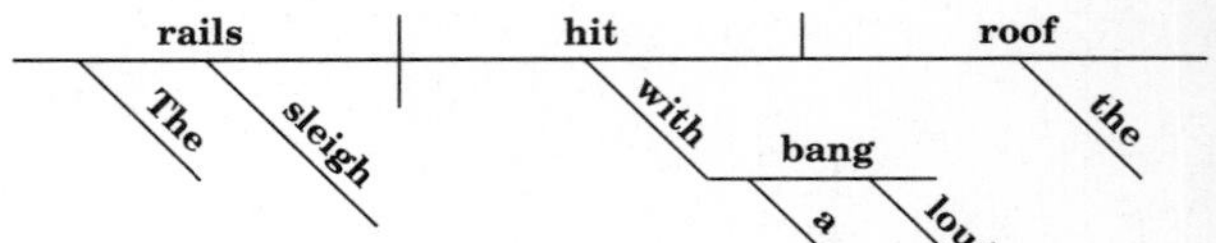 rails | hit | roof; The; sleigh; with bang; a; loud; the

4. 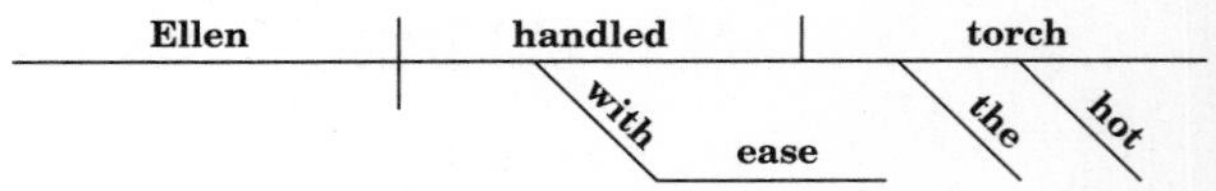 Ellen | handled | torch; with ease; the; hot

5. 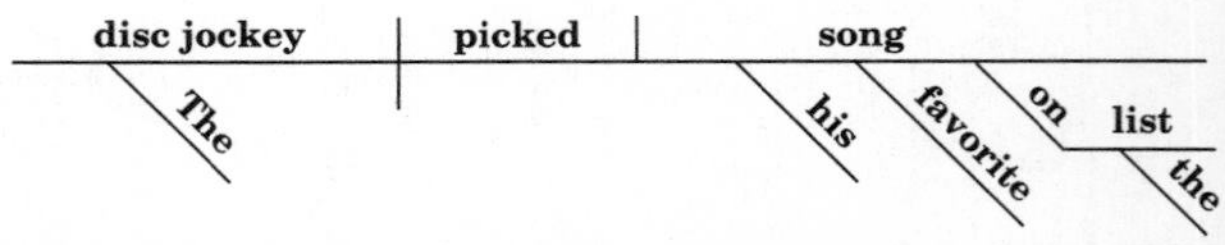 disc jockey | picked | song; The; his; favorite; on list; the

Answer Key

EXERCISE 1 — page 24

1\. She | gives | pain — me — a

2\. 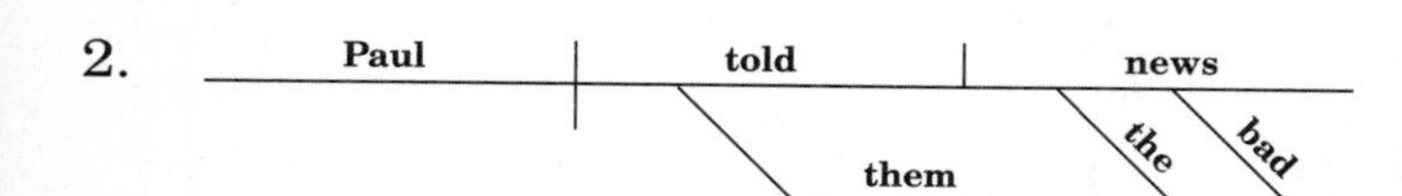

3\. 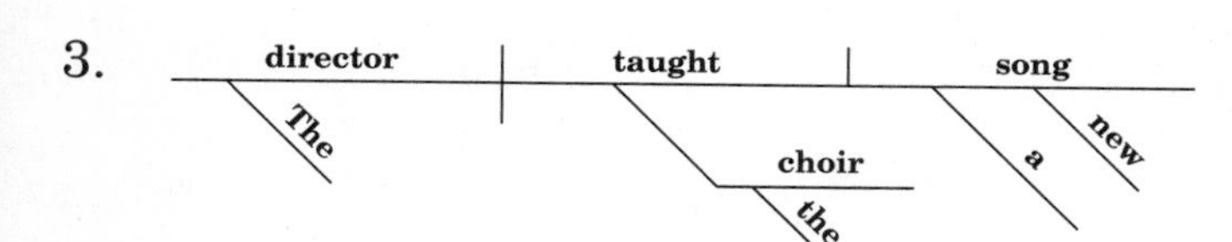

4\. 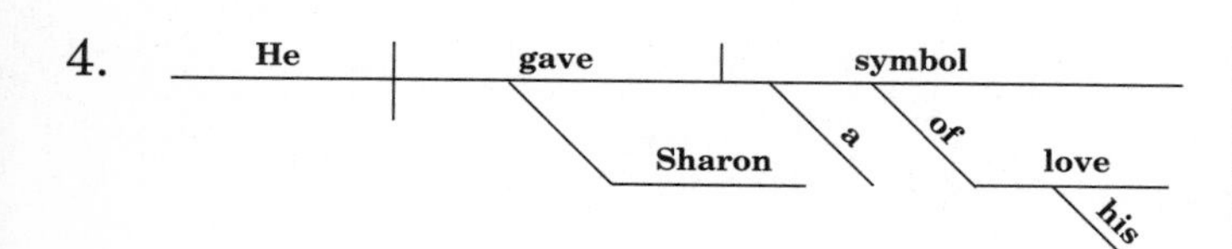

5\. 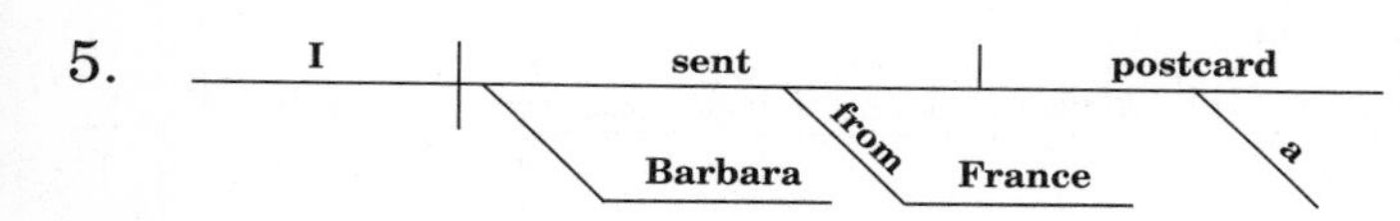

6\. 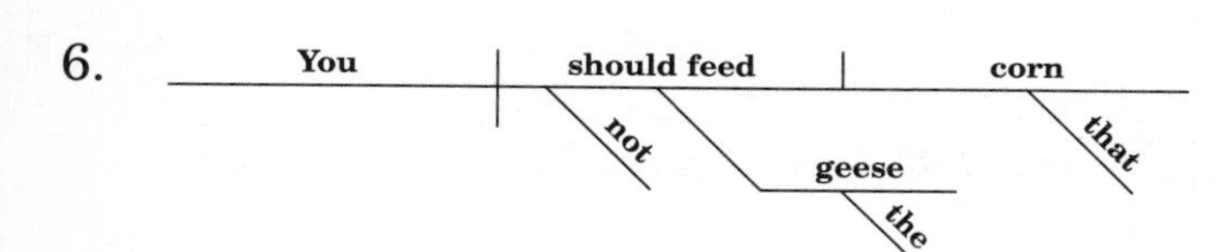

7\. 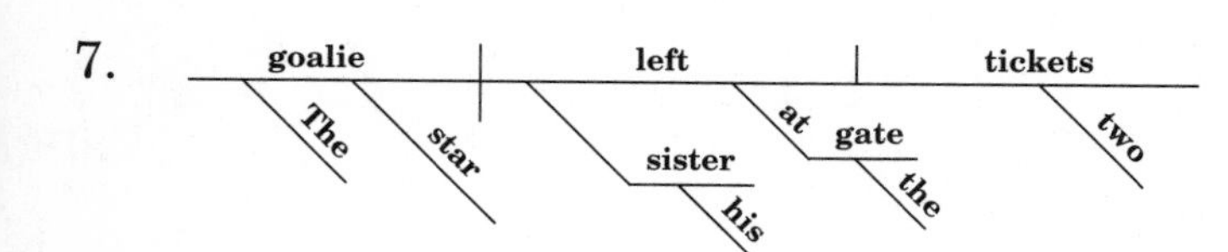

8\. 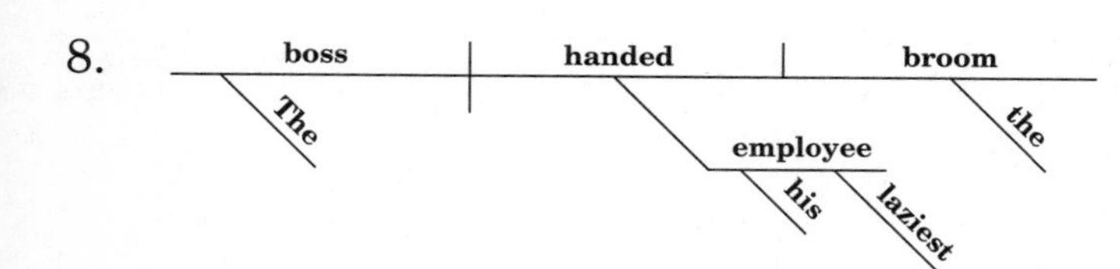

9\. 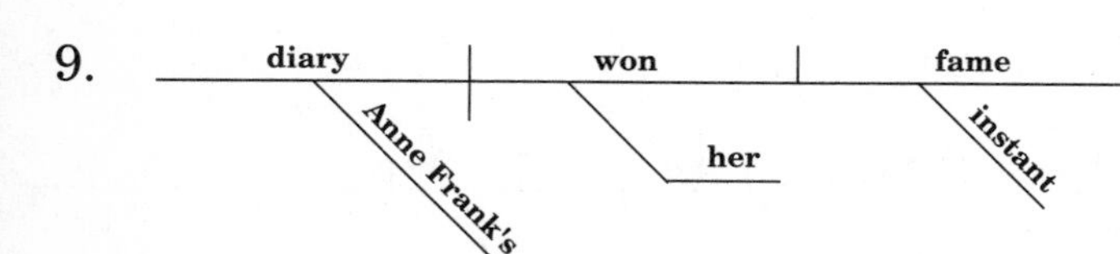

10\. 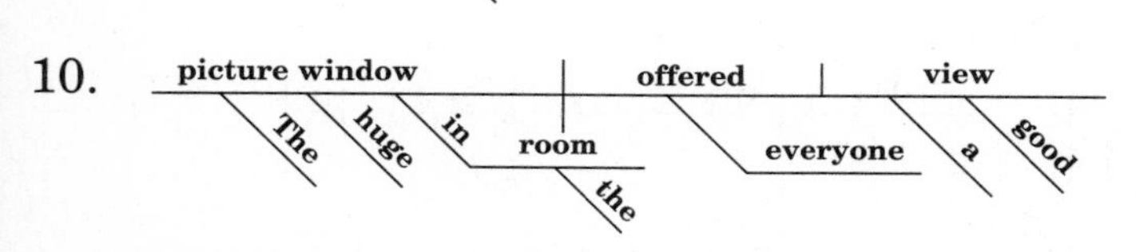

EXERCISE 2 — page 24 (Answers will vary)

EXERCISE 3 — page 25

1\. 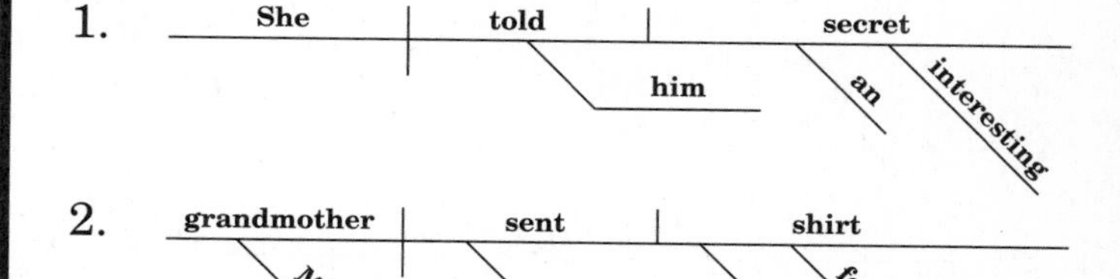

2\. grandmother | sent | shirt — My — me — a — for — Christmas

3\. 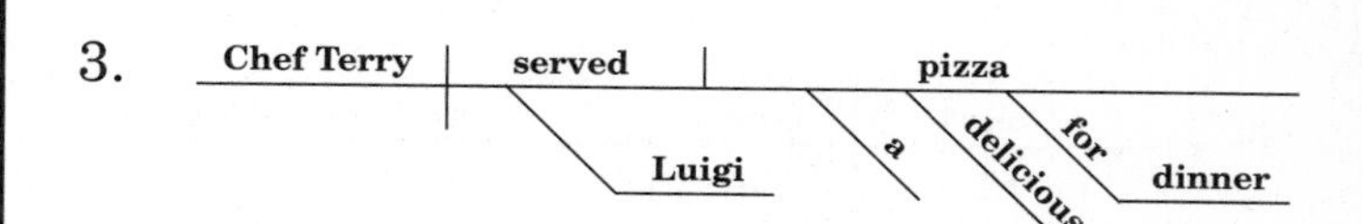

4\. 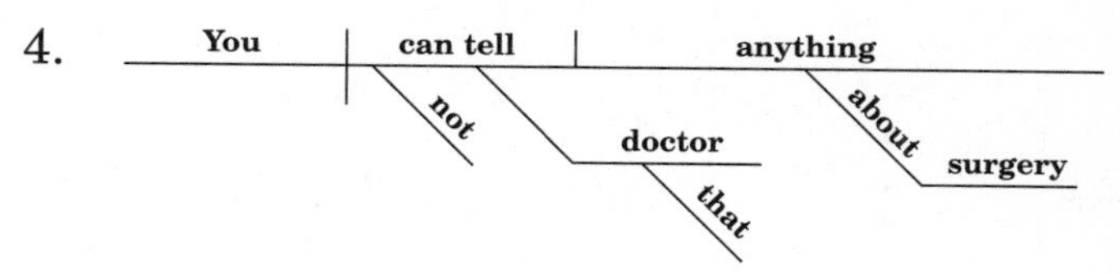

5\. 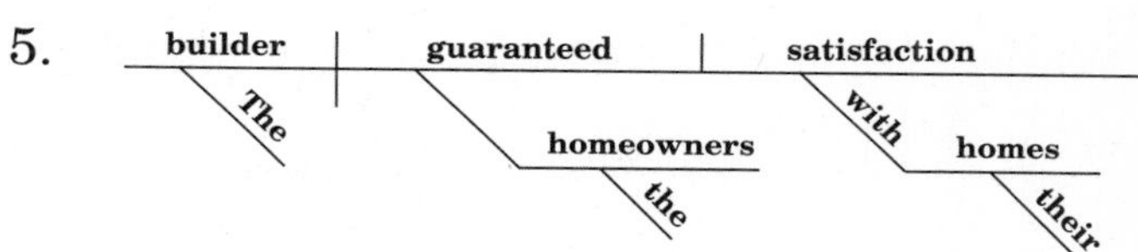

EXERCISE 4 — page 25

1\. 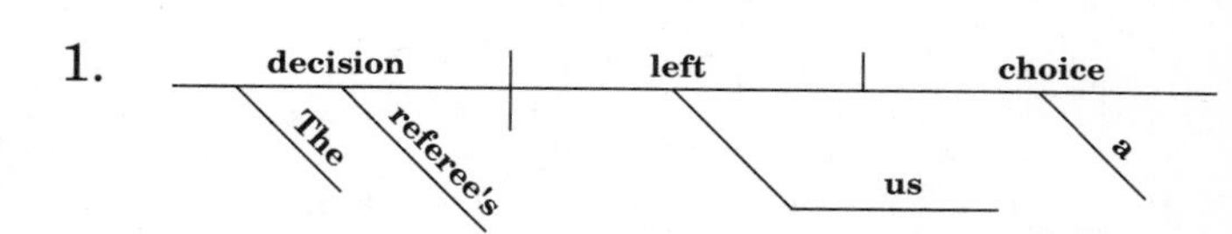

2\. 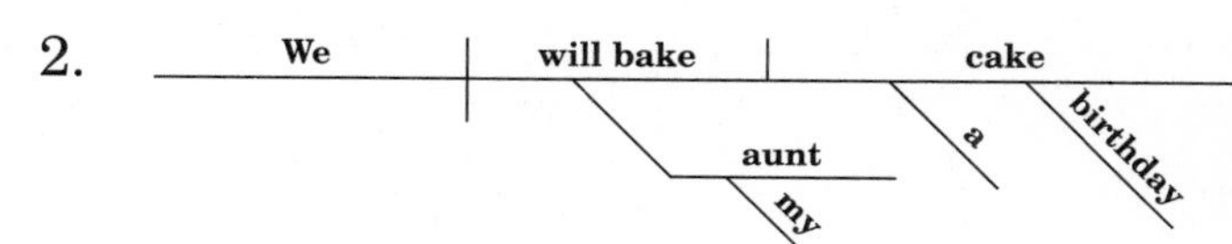

3\. 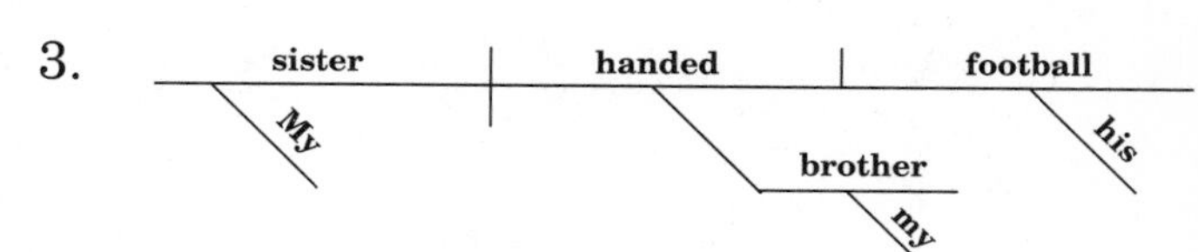

4\. 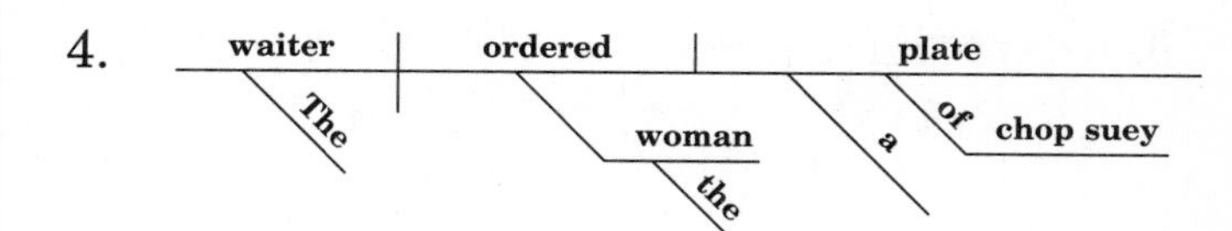

5\. 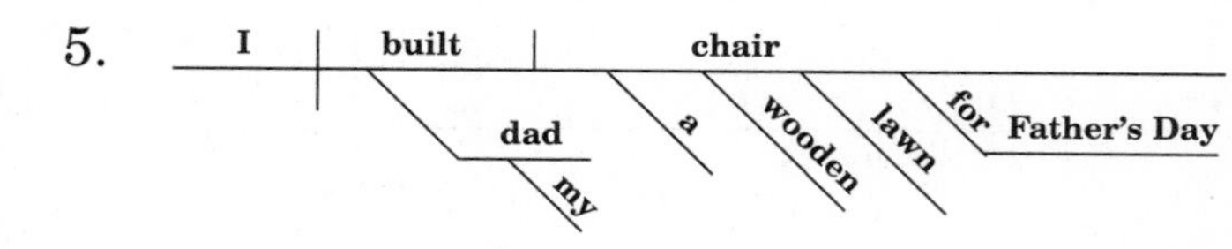

Answer Key

EXERCISE 1 — page 26

1.

They | made | Greg \ spokesman

for company

the

2. 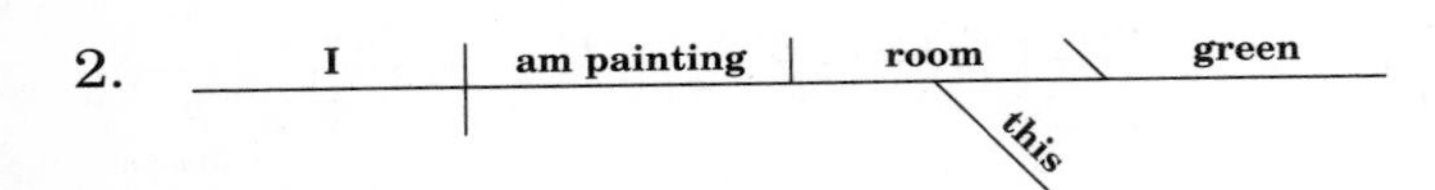

3. 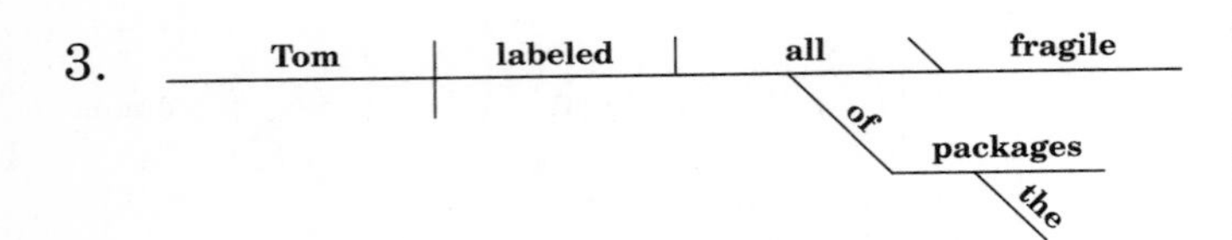

4. 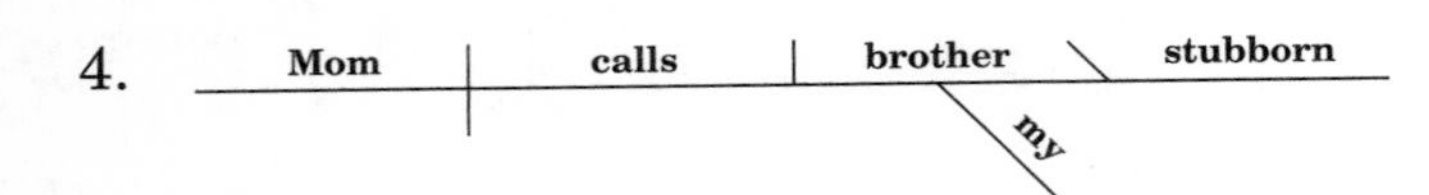

5.

We | will make | Heather \ goalie

6. 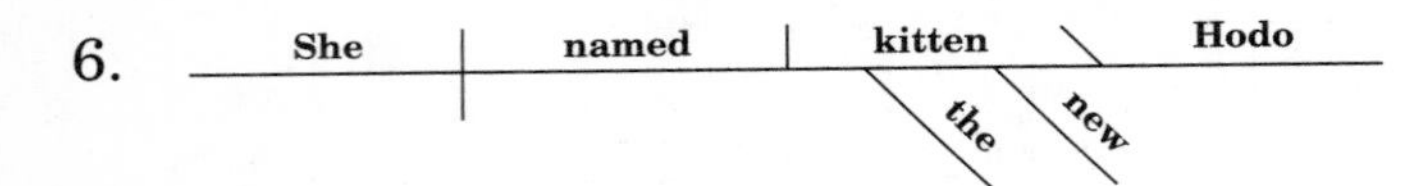

7. 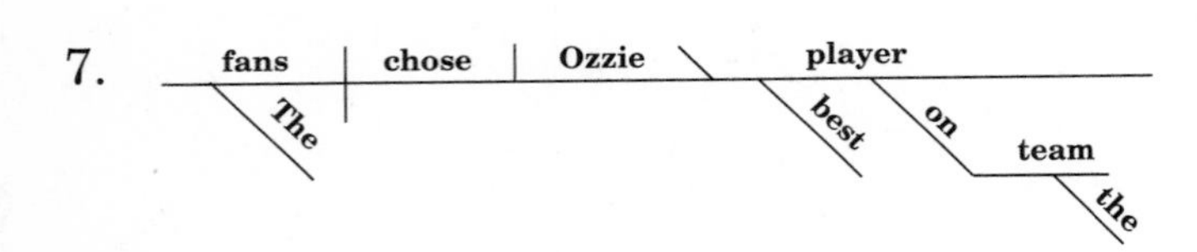

8. 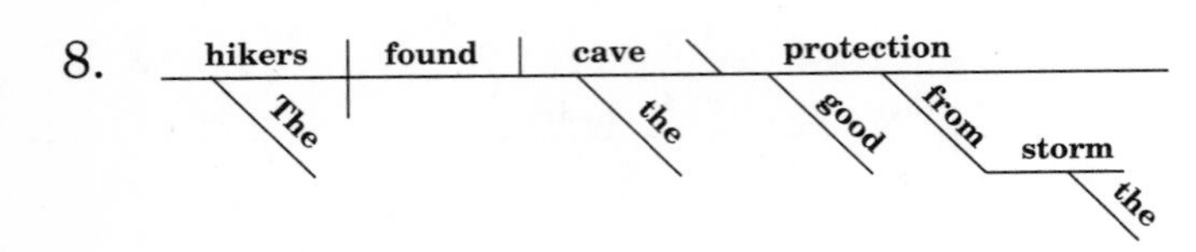

9. 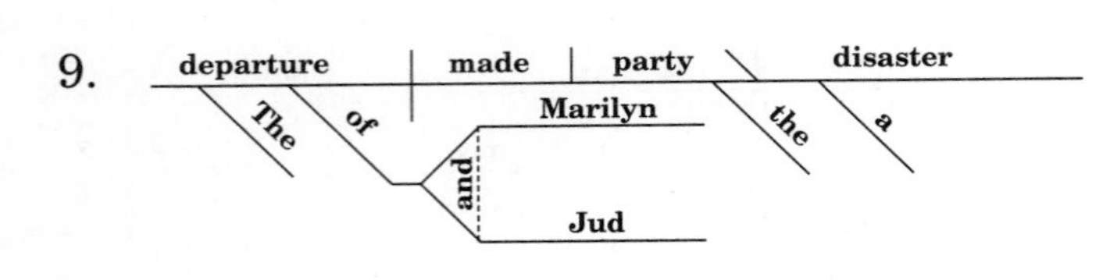

10.

Jim | finds | books \ worthwhile

all

EXERCISE 2 — page 26 (Answers will vary)

EXERCISE 3 — page 27

1. 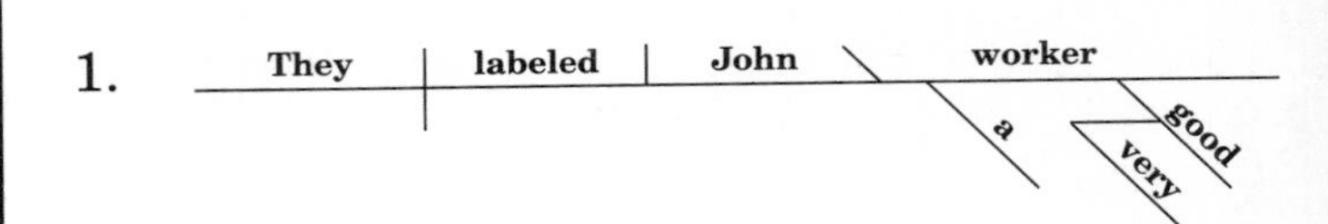

2. 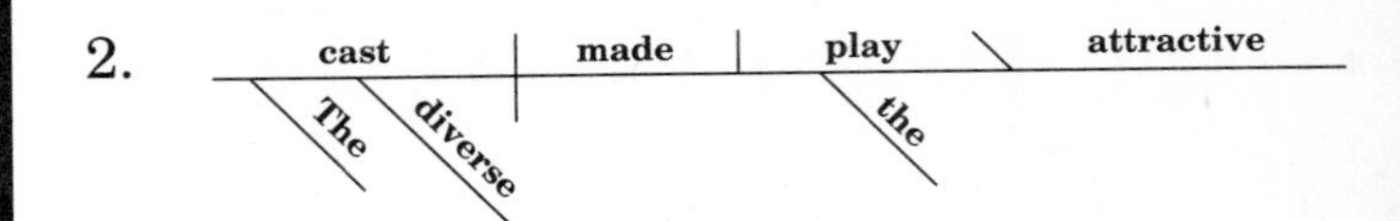

3. 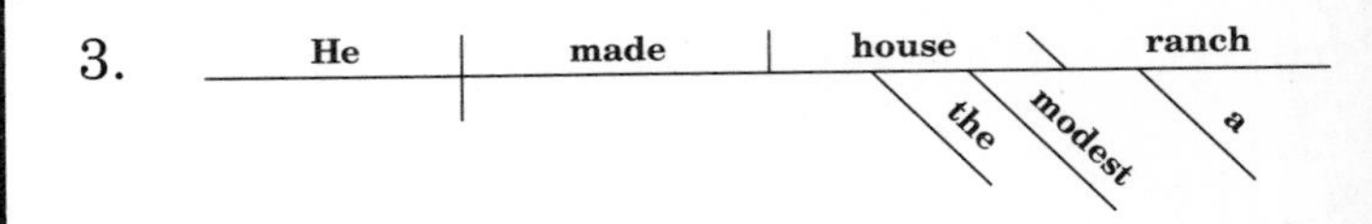

4. 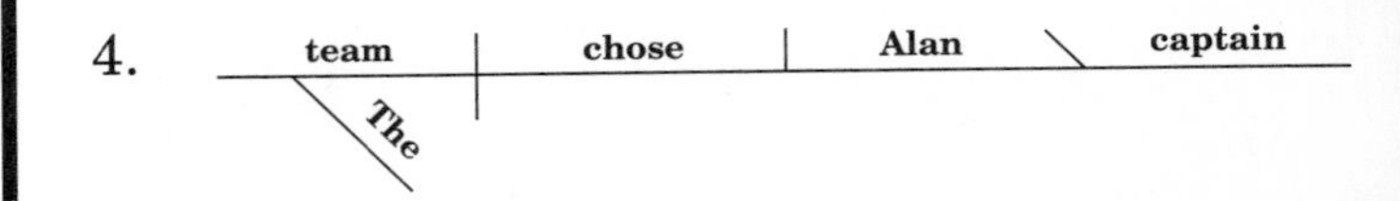

5.

Frank Lloyd Wright | called | building \ landmark

his an architectural

EXERCISE 4 — page 27

1. 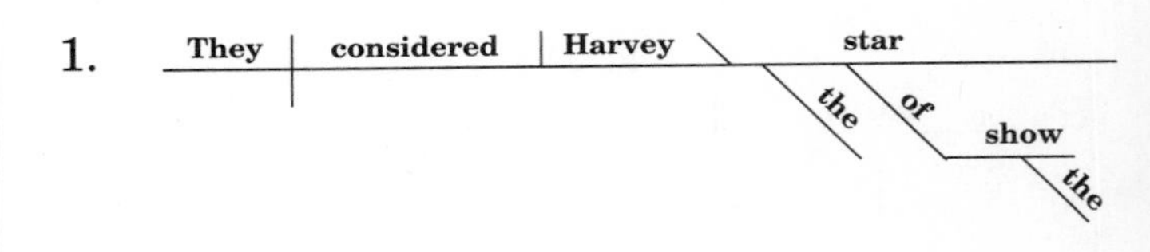

2. 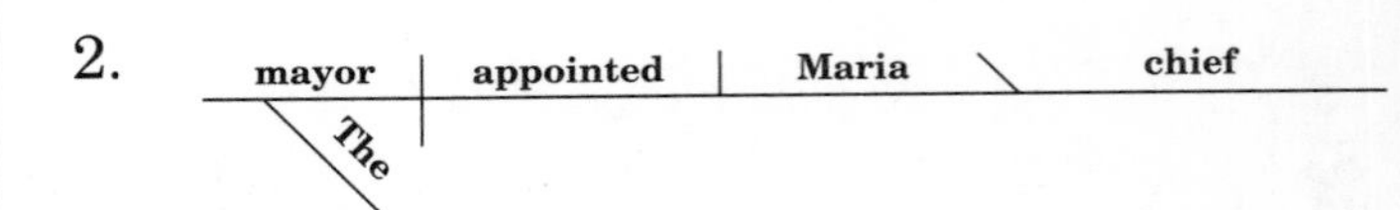

3. 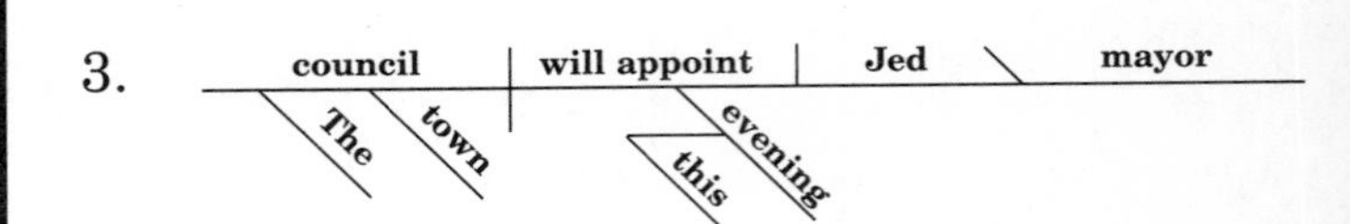

4. 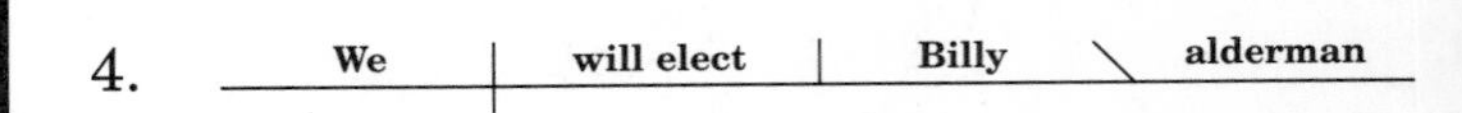

5. 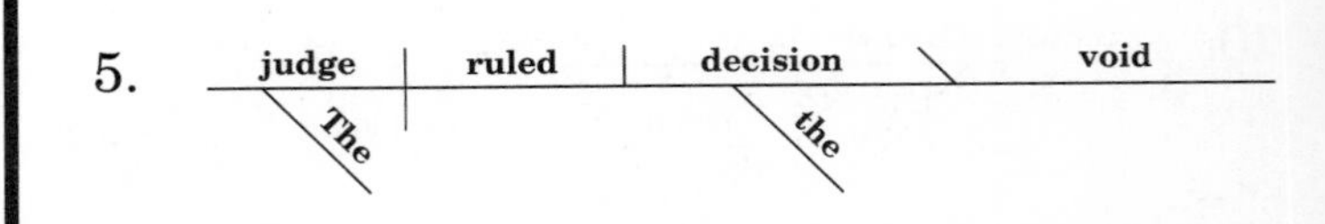

Answer Key

Compound Subjects Review — page 28

1. 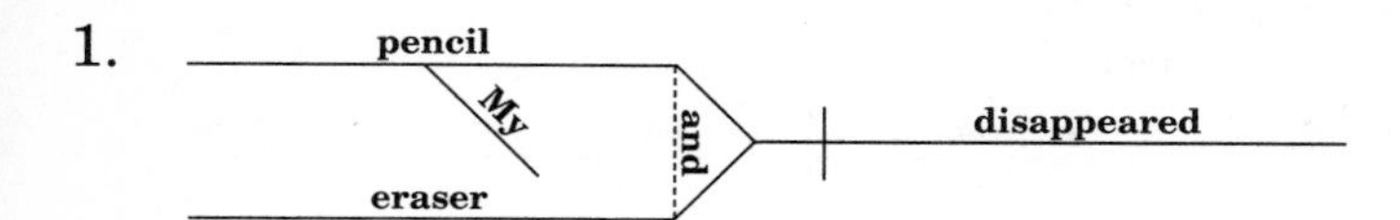

2. 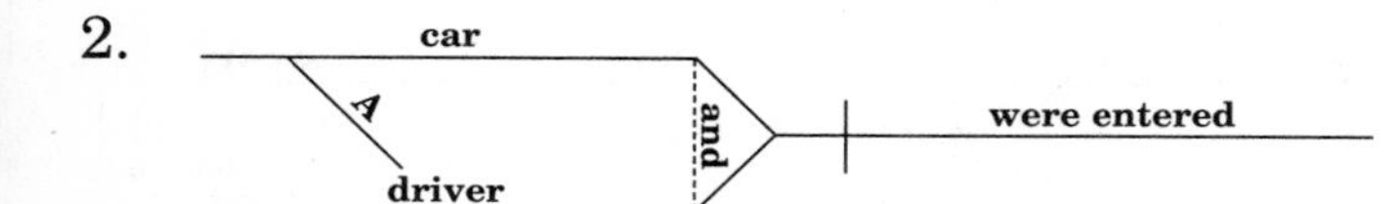

3. 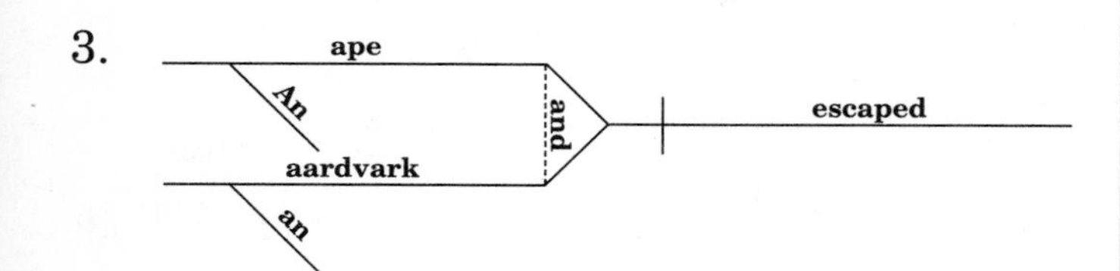

4. 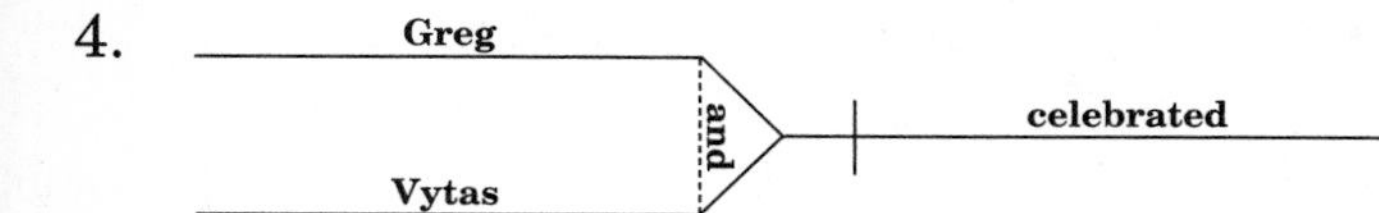

5. 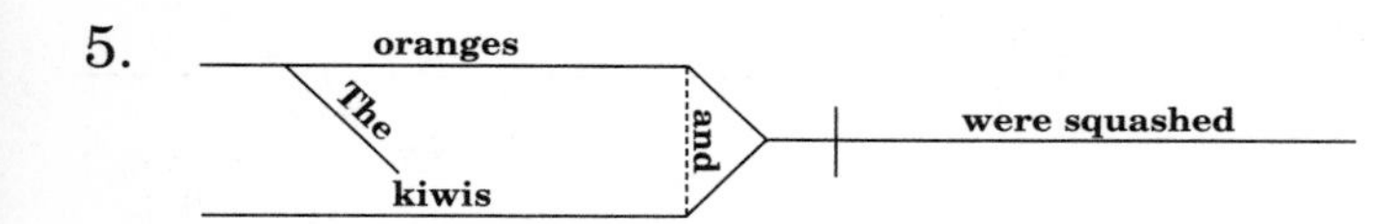

Compound Verb Review — page 28

1. 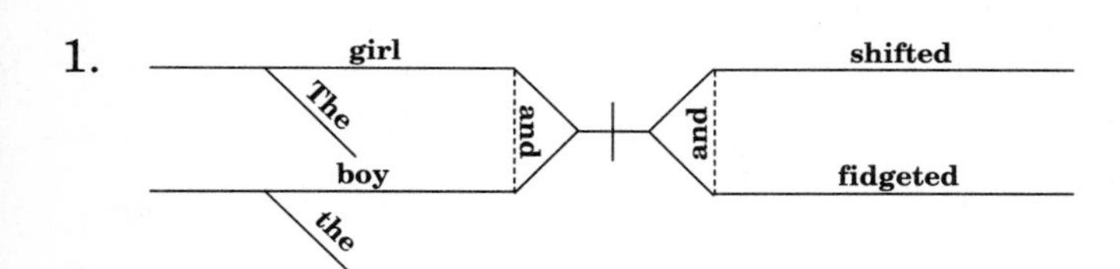

2. 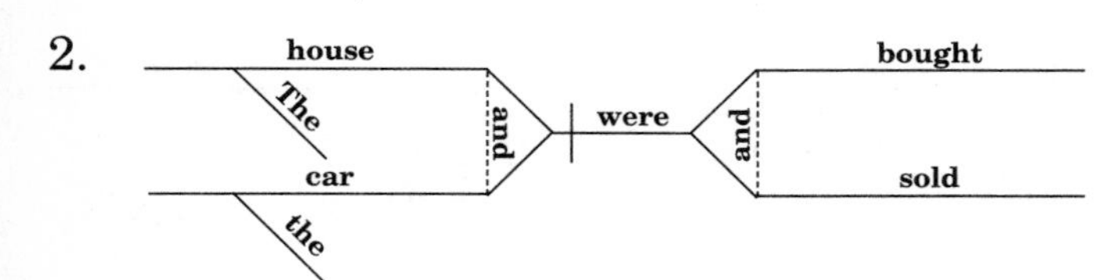

3. 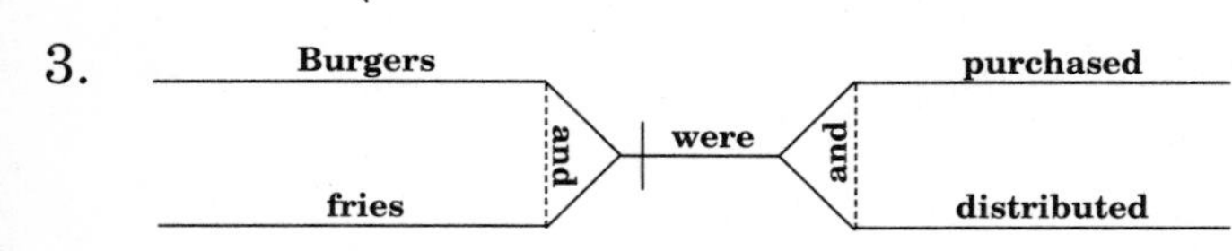

4. 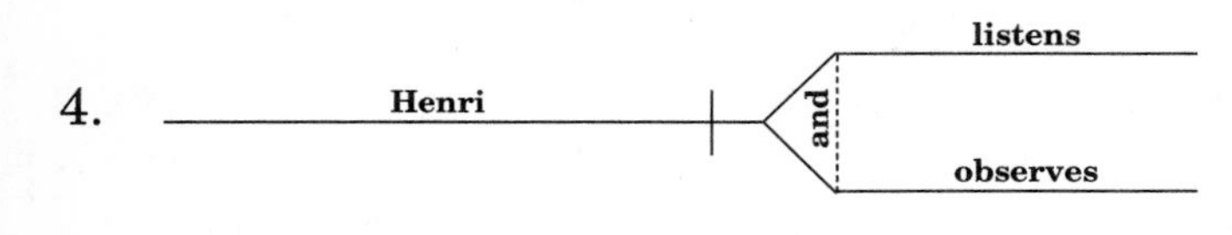

5. John | can | and | read | comprehend

Adjective Modifiers Review — page 29

1. 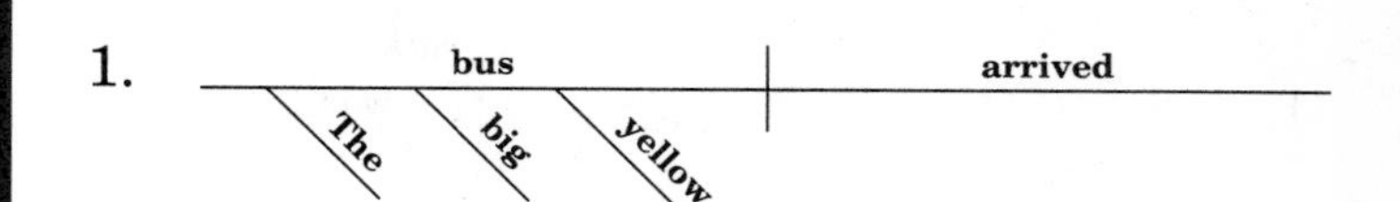

2. beans | will grow | Green

3. 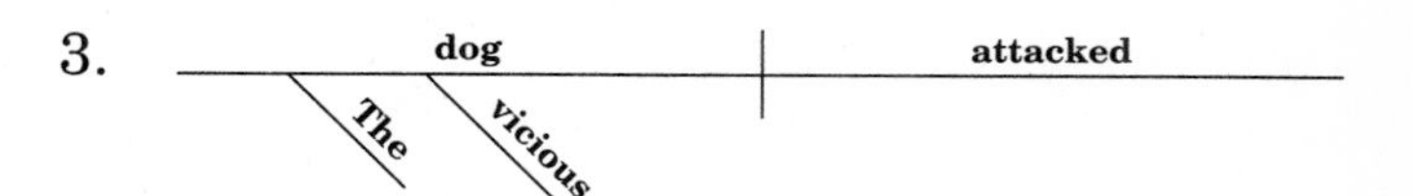

4. 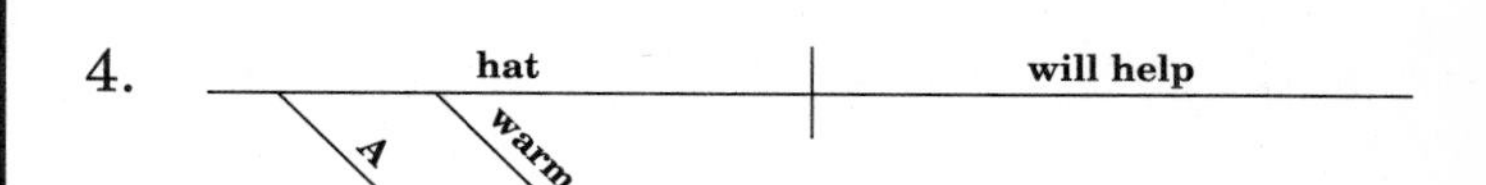

5. 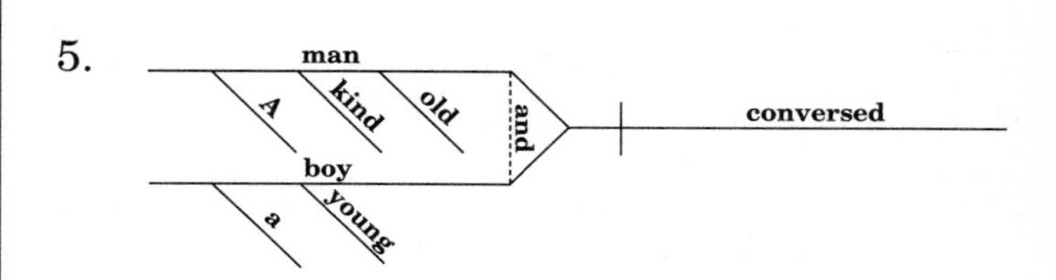

Adverb Modifiers Review — page 29

1. 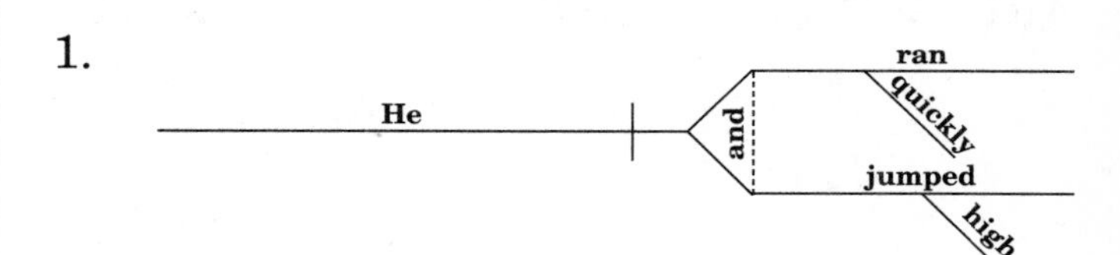

2. 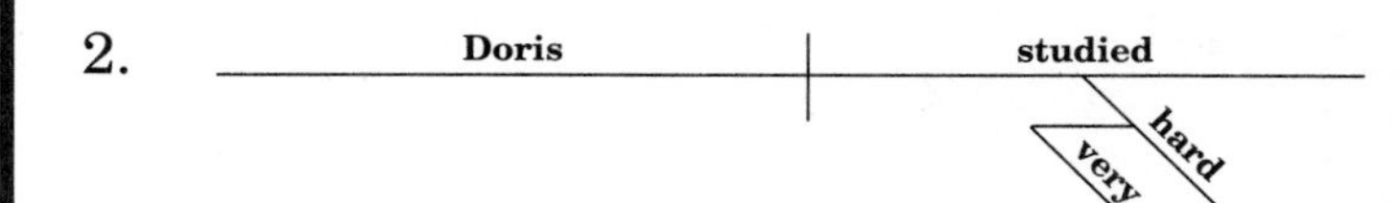

3. mouth | Her | small | round | opened | wide

4. gate | The | red | slammed | shut

5. 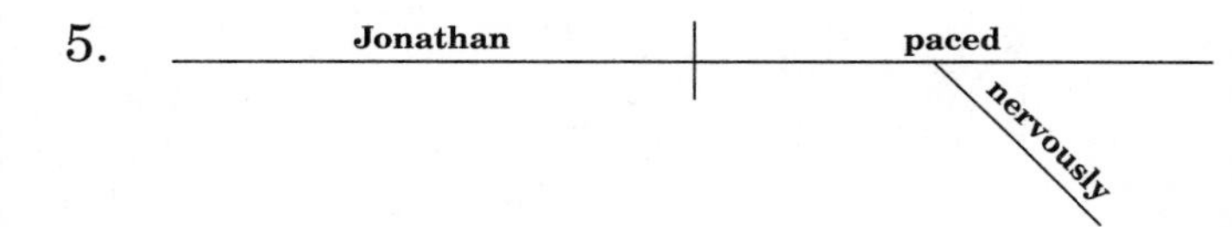

Answer Key

Adjective Prepositional Phrases — page 30

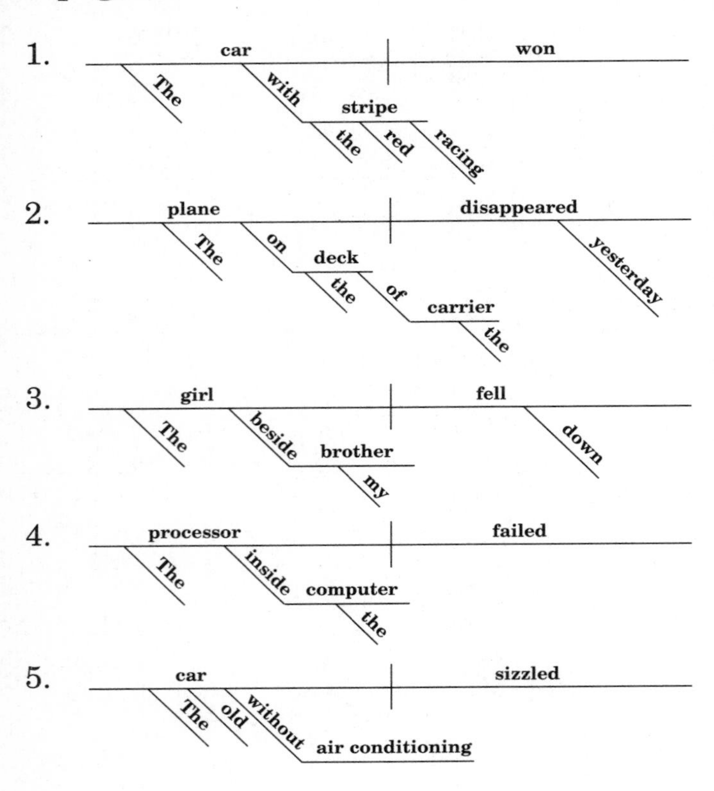

Adverb Prepositional Phrases — page 30

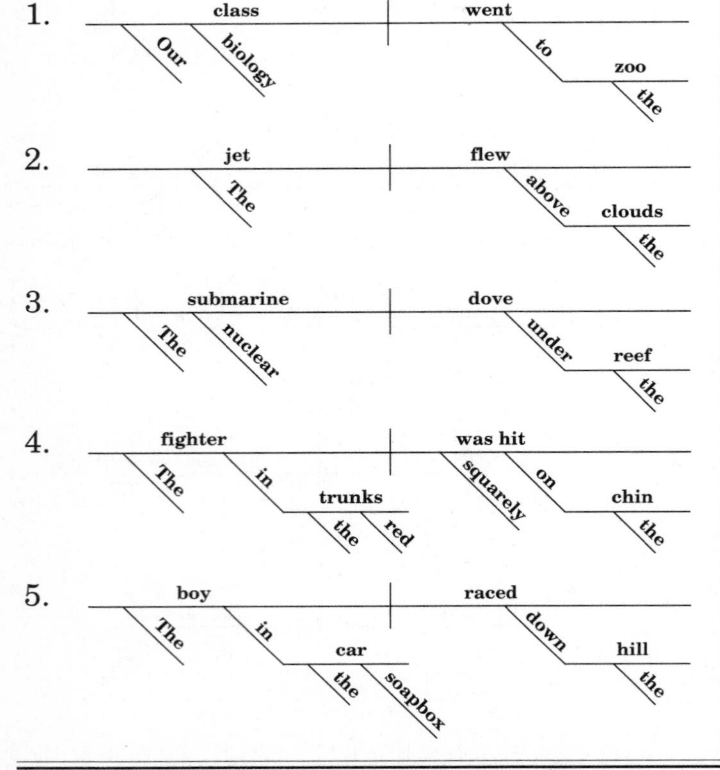

Subject Complements-Predicate Adjectives — page 31

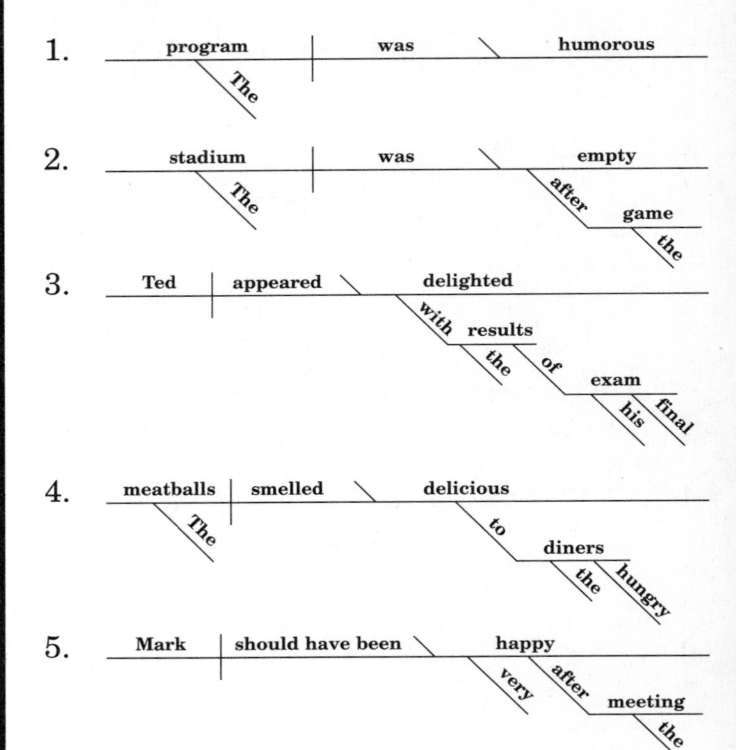

Subject Complements-Predicate Nouns — page 31

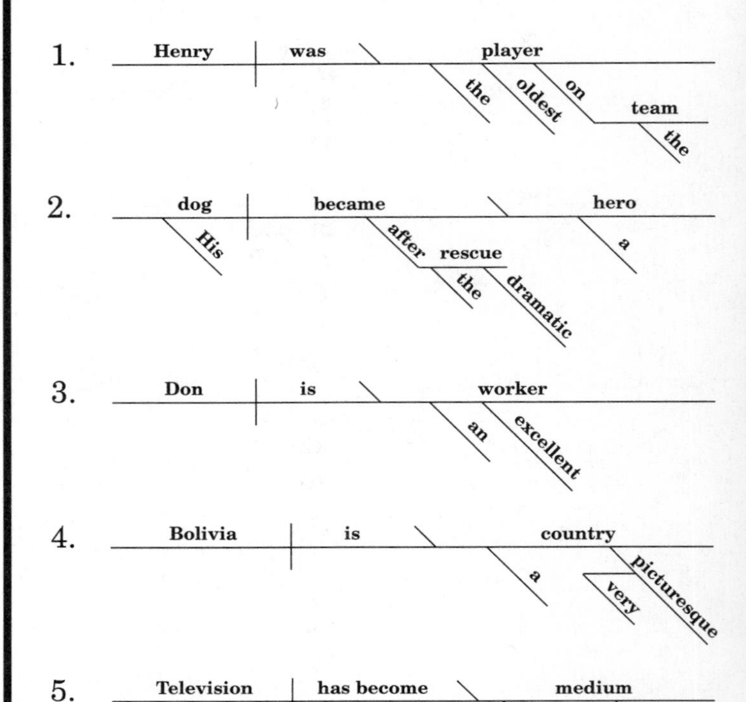